THE
VINTAGE DOG
SCRAPBOOK

- THE BLACK AND TAN
TERRIER -

British Library Cataloguing-in-Publication Data
A catalogue record for this book is available from
the British Library

VDB

www.vintagedogbooks.com

THE BLACK AND TAN TERRIER   NEW POND ANNABELLA

MY DOG

Here is a friend who proves his worth
Without conceit or pride of birth.
Let want or plenty play the host,
He gets the least and gives the most –
       He's just a dog.

He's ever faithful, kind and true;
He never questions what I do,
And whether I may go or stay,
He's always ready to obey
       'Cause he's a dog

Such meagre fare his want supplies!
A hand caress, and from his eyes
There beams more love than mortals know;
Meanwhile he wags his tail to show
       That he's my dog.

He watches me all through the day,
And nothing coaxes him away;
And through the night-long slumber deep
He guards the home wherein I sleep –
       And he's a dog.

I wonder if I'd be content
To follow where my master went,
And where he rode – as needs he must –
Would I run after in his dust
       Like other dogs.

How strange if things were quite reversed –
The man debased, the dog put first.
I often wonder how t'would be
Were he the master 'stead of me –
    And I the dog.

A world of deep devotion lies
Behind the windows of his eyes;
Yet love is only half his charm-
He'd die to shield my life from harm.
    Yet he's a dog.

If dogs were fashioned out of men
What breed of dog would I have been?
And would I e'er deserve caress,
Or be extolled for faithfulness
    Like my dog here?

As mortals go, how few possess
Of courage, trust, and faithfulness
Enough from which to undertake,
Without some borrowed traits, to make
    A decent dog!
                    - JOSEPH M. ANDERSON

DON'T CALL A MAN A DOG

WHEN we consider how loyal the dog is, even to an evil, cruel master . . . .

WHEN we consider how patient the dog is in this hurly-burly world of ours . . . .

WHEN we consider how the dog possesses the cardinal virtue we humans lack most-to forgive fully. . . .

WHEN we consider how the dog enters wholeheartedly into whatever task is assigned him, unpleasant though it may be . . . .

WHEN we consider that man is the most selfish, designing creature on earth and his dog the most unselfish living thing in the world, risking even life without hesitation . . . .

WHEN we consider how the dog lives a wholesome philosophy of enjoying every passing moment, finding daily delight in living, and to his dying day, retaining a heart of youth . . . .

WHEN we consider how, in the home, the dog by practice and self-example, is a teacher to children and grownups of such qualities as responsibility, obedience, kindness and social altruism . . . .

WHEN we consider all these things and that the dog is the nearest approach on earth to the actual living of the teachings of Jesus of Nazareth . . . .

WHEN we consider all these things – DON'T CALL A MAN A DOG – IT'S UNFAIR TO THE DOG.

MANCHESTER TERRIER : Champion *Stone Pits Judy*, the property of Mr. A. Baxendale of 11 Stone Pits, Edenfield, Nr. Manchester.

"FOR RICHER, FOR POORER"

I had a mansion fine; for once
Men said I "rolled in riches;"
Grand paintings hung around its walls,
And statues filled its niches.

The horses in my stable large
Were sleek, well fed, and glossy;
And chief among my dogs I loved
A silken pet, named Flossy.

He dined off fish and fowl and flesh;
By Dukes and Lords was patted;
His wavy coat was daily combed,
And never once seen matted.

He slept on downy satin couch
Within my chamber nightly;
And walked with me o'er velvet lawns,
Whene'er the sun shone brightly.

But ah! there came to me one day
A change most unexpected,-
My wealth took flight, and I was poor,
And homeless, and dejected!

My friends – if *friends* they might be called –
They left me altogether;
Just as the swallows fly away
At chill of wintry weather.

And turning to my dog, I said,
"I leave this house tomorrow;
Will *you* desert me, like the rest,
Or come and share my sorrow?"

The faithful creature licked my hand,
With full eyes overflowing,
That seemed to say, "Your lot is mine;
I go where *you* are going."

We left the place, my dog and I, -
The park-gates closed behind us;
The servants all too busy seemed
To say farewell, or mind us.

We took a cottage, snug and small,
Outside a distant village,
And furnished it too humbly far
For thief to plan its pillage.

I till my own trim garden now.
My dog is ever near me;
He races round the little lawn,
And does his best to cheer me.

I cannot say that *now* he feasts
On food in wasteful measure;
He eats his biscuit hard, and hides
Dry bones as men hide treasure.

And though his coat is never combed,
And looks not fine and glossy,
A dog more full of life and joy
'Twere hard to find than Flossy.

Beside my humble bed at night
He drags a woolly mat in,
And seems to sleep as soundly there
As on a couch of satin.

And oft I say, "My dog! I feel
As if with man disgusted;
The *you*, of all my seeming friends,
Were *only* to be trusted."

- MRS. SURR

COURAGE AND COWARDICE

The wind was rough, the wild waves broke
In thunder on the shore,
As swift a frightened cur rushed by,
Half scared at Ocean's roar.

Through furtive glances at the sea
His eyes their white revealed;
With tail between his legs he ran,
As though his doom were sealed!

Scared from our ears had died away
The lean cur's piteous whine,
When forth a grand retriever sprang
In haste to breast the brine.

A splendid plunge he made for stick,
Flung far in surging tide;
And battling with the crested waves,
Brought back his prize with pride.

O cowardice, we thought, how mean
In man or beast thou art!
But noble courage claims the praise
Of every youthful heart.

No child, however young and small,
But may a hero be;
Hard battles he may fight and win
Upon his bended knee.

For prayer will chase a thousand foes-
Bad tempers, malice, pride;
And, in the strength of God, the hosts
Of hell may be defied.

And soon the happy time shall come
When fighting shall be o'er,
And all the joyful conquerors crowned
Upon the heavenly shore.

- MRS. SURR

My Dog is Dead

There lies his ball; I wait to see him pounce
And shake it in mock fight which pleases him.
I thought I heard his quick light step again
In playful trot on stairway up and down.

The leash hangs on the wall; I'll shake it loud,
Then joyfully he'll bound into the room
Impatient for his romp. He does not come-
No wistful face peers through half-open door.

The rugs lie smooth; the curtains are not torn.
I haven't missed a shoe or rag today.
The house is dreadfully still, until I wish
I heard four feet come pitpat down the hall.

The soft moist nose that pushed against my hand
The paw that touched me to demand its wish,
The pleading lively eye, the plaintive bark-
What sweet annoyances they now would seem!

The door is open and the gate ajar;
No need to close them-he will not run out.
The new ball throw away; I bought it for
His next birthday-but he will never know.

The Old Dog

The old dog sleeps before the fire
Content to doze the hours away.
His step now drags uncertainly
Where once he frisked 'mid bark and play

Long lies he in the warming sun-
The hunter home from faroff hills,
To run his last and losing race
As eyes grow dim and legs give way.

Keen life still clings within his frame
Yet 'tis but trace of other days
As memory's musings run the chase
In years when legs were swift and strong.

He's deep asleep while muffled bark,
The twitching nose and treading feet
Waft him in dreams across the fields
On trails of game and new-found scent.

Tonight you softly pat his head
As blinking eyes are quick to close.
You miss his wonted nudge and park
When morning finds him still asleep.

You call-he does not open eye
Or wag that ever cheerful tail;
You think him merely sleeping sound-
And soon to leap up joyfully.

Alas, the stiff and stretched out legs,
The breathless loin, the glassy eye
Which oft so soft and moist did plead,
Tell now that death has found its mark!

The brave, stout heart beats now no more
To warm the body whose sole thot
Knew only your command as law-
A servant for your ev'ry wish.

A noble soul has fled the earth,
Which never knew deceit nor guile;
Of man was part, a better part,
Without his treach'rous smile and face.

High up at heaven's gate he waits
Without complaint though long the hours-
An ear pricked up, half-opened eye
To catch quick sight when master comes.

At last a loved familiar face
The watchful dog discerns with joy.
"What sound is that?" the master asks
In strange surprise. No need to wait-

The answer comes in leap and bark-
Old dog, old master once again
Unite to never part as both
In gladsome pace wend way to God.

BLACK-AND-TAN TERRIER, FROM PICTURE BY SARTORIUS.

Dogs, Too, Get Spring Fever

In all lands the return of warming sunshine brings the pleasing spring fever. Dogs too are its willing victims. They find increasing delight in their daily vagabonding. The plain, soft earth after a winter of concealment under the snow, presents myriads of new smells; and as anyone initiated into the inner cult of dog lore can tell you, the hors d'oeuvres of a canine menu are the multitude of smells awaiting detection by the dog's nose in every spot and space.

The paws of the dog itch to be soothed by digging in the once-again soft ground of springtime. A neighbour's lawn has just been dedicated with the planting of flower seeds and shrubbery after a winter of ecstatic reading of the alluring seed catalogues by the hopeful neighbour.

Beware-you will incur your good neighbour's enmity! Act before it is too late! Be certain that your dog harkens to your voice, else you will need to retrieve him in the front yard next door happily scratching up the earth and grass with all fours and looking at you with a devil-may-car, "haven't we got fun?" expression.

It's his forgivable way of expressing spring fever. But-call him quickly and hide yourself away before your neighbour's wife spots you out of the front window. Walk nonchalantly as if you never owned a dog in your life.

And have your wife send to your neighbour's wife that evening as a peace offering, some delicacy she has just cooked, for dogs will be dogs, especially in springtime.

The Dog's Bill of Rights

I.   I want nutritious food once daily-not too much; and don't believe the old idea that bones are good for me.

II.   I want clean water in a clean dish twice daily.

III.   I want a dry, ventilated but draftless place for sleeping.

IV.   I want a collar that doesn't choke me or isn't so loose it catches on my head.

V.   I want a quiet place in the basement on the Fourth of July

VI.   I want every boy reprimanded but softly, who throws stones at me or twists my ears.

VII.   I want folks to judge me as a dog and from a dog's viewpoints.

VIII.   I want everybody to keep in mind that I do with my mouth, most things they do with their hands; so, they needn't be afraid of a dog's teeth.

IX.   I want to be treated sympathetically, just as I treat small children and all those in distress, who belong to my master's clan.

X.   I want my mind and body trained so that I can be of the fullest service.

XI.   I want to be considered one of the family, for I will give my life to protect it.

XII.   I want my master to be my god on earth and to act the part.

SIGNED: for all dogs:

FIDO

Seventeen Training Don'ts

Sometimes what should be done can be said best by telling what should not be done. The reasons for the don'ts should be evident to every person in process of training his dog. Each one is based upon the basic psychology of the dog's mind.

1. Don't punish your dog while you are angry or lack control of yourself.
2. Don't punish your dog with the lead or any instrument of training or anything he should associate with duty or pleasure.
3. Don't sneak up on your dog, grab him from the rear, surprise him or reach for him quickly.
4. Don't chase your dog to catch him; he must come to you or follow after you.
5. Don't coax your dog to you and then turn upon him with punishment. You will regret the deception.
6. Don't trick, fool or taunt your dog. It is cruel and inconsistent to tease your dog to come to you when he can not.
7. Don't punish a dog by stepping on his paws needlessly. They are exceedingly sensitive. Don't twist his ears playfully or otherwise. Don't strike him on the backbone, in the face or on the ears.
8. Don't nag your dog; don't be giving orders to him constantly; don't pester him with your shoutings.

9. Don't praise a dog for doing a certain act, then at a later time scold him for doing the same act. Consistency on your part is a chief virtue in dog training.
10. Don't train your dog within an hour after he has eaten.
11. Don't ever lose patience with a puppy younger than six months and seldom with a dog older.
12. Don't throw or kick a puppy nor lift him by the head or leg or skin of the neck.
13. Don't work your dog without some short rest or play periods during training lesson. A five-minute rest for every twenty minutes of training is desirable. Feats requiring strength and endurance are for a dog older than six months.
14. Don't permit everyone and anyone to give commands to your dog. While you are training him, he must be a one-man dog, depending on you to feed him and care for him.
15. Don't consider tricks the chief purpose in training. Usefulness is the object sought in all instruction of the dog. Acts that spring naturally from the dog's instincts are to be fostered.
16. Don't expect your dog to be a wonderful dog after a few weeks of training; four months to a year may be necessary in order to make the master proud of him, but the work is worth the effort. Training never ends.
17. Don't jump to the conclusion that your dog is dumb. He may differ with you, believing the trainer should know more than the dog.

30 DON'TS FOR EVERY DOG OWNER

Don't surprise a sleeping dog nor approach any dog without giving him notice.

Don't make a sissy of your dog by coddling him.

Don't allow the dog to become chilled after bathing.

Don't give worm medicine to a sick dog.

Don't exercise the dog within thirty minutes after he has eaten.

Don't allow strangers to chastise the dog.

Don't fear a dog merely because he is frothing at the mouth.

Don't allow the dog to lie constantly near the radiator in winter.

Don't fondle or pet strange dogs.

Don't give quantities of water to a dog that is vomiting.

Don't allow dogs to sit in any and all chairs in the home.

Don't take dogs needlessly into strange kennels as there is danger of disease.

Don't allow the dog to roam by himself; he should always be within sight of his master.

Don't beat a dog; a light stroke with a few loosely rolled sheets of newspaper plus shaming with the voice generally are sufficient.

Don't believe that eating of meat by the dog will make it "go mad."

Don't give castor oil for all forms of constipation.

Don't neglect paying (and promptly too) for damages your dog may have done.

Don't pour kerosene on a dog's skin for killing fleas.

Don't neglect calling a veterinarian promptly for your sick dog since both dog and doctor want to live.

Don't encourage needless dog fights.

Don't attempt to take a bone away from a dog without first calling his attention to yourself; never interfere with a strange dog while it is eating.

Don't feed any very small or sharp-pointed bones.

Don't let your dog sleep in a draft or in a damp place.

Don't let everybody pet your dog if he is to be a watchdog.

Don't shout commands to your dog in an excited tone of voice.

Don't kill your dog by overfeeding him.

Don't run the risk of losing your dog by not having your name and address on his collar plate.

Don't try to avoid paying a dog license fee.

Don't let your dog cross the street without being by your side, even if well trained, or on lead.

Don't believe everything poorly informed people tell you about dogs.

Type of Black-and-Tan Terrier.—Mr. Higgs's strain.

A Dozen Dog Care Do's

1. Trim toenails every three months with heavy scissors or regular nail trimmer.
2. Have a set day each month for examining your dog externally inch by inch, including "smelling the ears."
3. Brush or wipe the teeth and gums with a soft cloth weekly and weakly, either dry or slightly soaked in salt-and soda water solution.
4. Watch the frequency, colour and consistency of bowel movements as symptom of ailing condition.
5. Feed your dog each day at the same scheduled hour and spot, and in the same food pan.
6. Brush your dog with a not-too-soft brush vigorously every day, no matter how lazy you yourself feel.
7. Take your dog and yourself out for three romps a day, one of which should be extra long.
8. Keep our dog, no matter how well trained, on a lead and close to you, (on your left) when on busy streets and in crowds.
9. Sun and air the dog's bedding once a week.
10. Cure a skin disease at first notice and before it has a chance to intensify.
11. Prolong your dog's life by keeping him away from the dinner table at mealtime and from eating frequently.
12. Have patience with your dog just as he 'puts up' with you. Be sympathetic with his limitations.

The Dog Gives Training Advice to His Master

Now, look here, human; I realize you've got to know more than the dog before you can teach him, but please mix common sense and good judgment with your knowledge.

I can't talk with words. You can teach me to lie down with the command UP. The big job you have in this training work with me as your pupil is to get your ideas across to me. Don't worry about my end of it, if I can figure out in my dog mind what you want me to do.

And incidentally, nine times of ten a dog disobeys, he isn't actually dong that-he just doesn't get what you had in mind. Believe me, we dogs have only one big act on our program-to win your approval in everything we do. I know it's misplaced devotion at times but we'll skip that.

Just remember, master, that we are dogs-and glad of it too. We aren't humans and don't want to be. To us this is a dog's world, mostly of smells and sounds. We don't want to be called humans-that's unfair to us.

But when you map out a training course look at it from the dog's viewpoint. Does the act appeal to our love of play, our desire to please our interest in getting something to eat, our curiosity in seeing what's happening on the other side of the fence> Put a canine angle on your training efforts-and we'll respond. We want to be all dog, and not half human.

Do you recall the famous court case in which Sam Smith was tried for shooting a dog that leaped over his fence, dug up his garden, and bit one of the Smith children badly? Well, the jury convicted Smith but we dogs took a vote and decided that the dog's owner should have been found guilty instead.

When one of us is taken to the pound in the dog catcher's truck and there murdered legally if no one reclaims us, our blood is no the soul of the owner who thought so little of us that he did not keep us under his control.

And why shouldn't we in turn set forth the essential qualities of a successful trainer? We want our trainers to possess an abundance of FOUR things:

1. Patience with its twin, self-control.
2. Seriousness of purpose, for the trainer is moulding our characters; and this seriousness demands that he concentrate on his training work similarly as he requires us.
3. Consistency of methods and aims, so that we will not be confused or deceived.
4. Sincere love for us dogs.

I might bark in passing that we laugh in our paw when you humans, our assumed gods, lose your temper over us, shout commands excitedly, are inconsistent in not sticking to the same command for the same obedience or let us get away with pretended deafness when you speak to us.

At any rate, just look at things through our eyes and minds; make yourself one of us for the time being when you are training us-you don't really train us-we can do all this sort of stuff naturally; you're just kind of dumb in getting it out of use.

Signed - - for all dogs, FIDO

A DOG'S TRAGEDY

On his morning rounds the Master
Goes to learn how all things fare;
Searches pasture after pasture,
Sheep and cattle eyes with care;
And, for silence or for talk,
He hath comrades in his walk;
Four dogs, each pair of different breed,
Distinguished two for scent, and two for speed.

See a hare before him started!
-Off they fly in earnest chase;
Every dog is eager-hearted,
All the four are in the race:
And the hare whom they pursue
Knows from instinct what to do;
Her hope is near: no turn she makes;
But, like an arrow, to the river takes.

Deep the river was, and crusted
Thinly by a one night's frost;
But the nimble hare hath trusted
To the ice, and safely crost;
She hath crost, and without heed
All are following at full speed,
When, lo! the ice, so thinly spread,
Breaks – and the greyhound, Dart, is over head!

Better fate have Prince and Swallow –
See them cleaving to the sport!
Music has no heart to follow,
Little Music, she stops short,
She hath neither wish nor heart,

Hers is now another part:
A loving creature she, and brave"
And fondly strives her struggling friend to save.

From the brink her paws she stretches,
Very hands as you would say!
And afflicting moans she fetches,
As he breaks the ice away.
For herself she hath no fears,-
Him alone she sees and hears,-
Makes efforts with complainings; nor gives o'er
Until her fellow sinks to reappear no more.
                              - WORDSWORTH

DOG LATIN

Eheu! hie jacet Crony,
A dog of much renown,
Nee fur, nee macaroni,
Though born and bred in town.

In war he was acerrimus,
In dog-like arts perite,
In love, alas! miserrimus,
For he died of a rival's bite.

His mistress struxit cenotaph;
And, as the verse comes pat in,
Ego qui scribo epitaph
Indite it in dog Latin.
                              - UNKNOWN

MR. E. A. SIMKIN'S BEADLE

BY THE SHERIFF——VIOLET LLOYD.

Cats versus Dogs

We like cats. They furnish running exercise for dogs and always win the race. They are a living, moving thing of beauty, softness and grace. They and the birds are among the few animals that wash themselves.

Like the dog, they are a heritage from the wilderness. But whereas Fido the dog has made an almost complete adjustment between savagery and civilisation, Pussy the cat clings to most of her ancestors' ways.

She is still a member of her ancient race of tigers, lions and panthers. She is a tiger of small size who deigns to favour you with her presence in your house, sleeping haughtily at your very fireplace. She permits you to occupy the house with her. Her lair demands her loyalty for she prefers it even though the family moves away.

She moves with all the proudness of her proud race. One would think that such diminutive descendant of the lion and the tiger would be marked with humility. Her very whiskers, pure relic of the jungle and its shadows, exude haughtiness. She washes herself publicly that all may see the rite of the elite.

She likes the darkness; her paths are those of the night; the starts evoke the melody of her soul (on these nocturnal romantic occasions, more commonly "his" soul).

She travels along. Who has seen a pack of cats? Secrecy confided to no one, is her abiding trait.

Behind those greenish-yellow gleaming eyes, guarded by pupils now round, no but an upright slit, reside mystery, adventure, and dark plannings.

She possesses a most uncertain disposition. Her set countenance starting at your face shamelessly may mean friendliness or a scratch. That gracefully agile tail may be but a salute to those about to die. She is a daughter of many moods, royal in her fits of temper.

Where the cat is a pet, the dog is a companion. Where the cat is a lady, the dog is a roustabout. Where the cat is disdainful, the dog is a good fellow. Where the cat is unconcerned with its mistress, the dog imitates the moods of his master.

We use "she" when speaking of cats but refer to the dog as "he" and could there be more conclusive proof of what we are trying to argue than this natural choice of pronoun in the third person.

THE FRIEND OF MAN

With eye upraised his master's look to scan,
The joy, the solace, and the aid of man;
The rich man's guardian and the poor man's friend,
The only creature faithful to the end.
                                    UNKNOWN

Have a Heart, Mr. Dog Owner

The following written by the author applies to the puppy just purchased, perhaps from a distant kennel, and now arrived in the home of its new owner. Most puppies are purchased "at a distance," and at the tender age of about four months.

NOTHING is more pathetic and at the same time more courageous than a few-months-old puppy literally pulled away from its mother, from its brothers and sisters; then pushed into a crate, shaken upon a jolting journey, finally to be ushered into the presence of strangers in its new home, whose selection certainly has been without its choice or knowledge.

THE SLATS are torn off the crate – a commotion enough to terrify even an old dog. The little breathing bunch of softness is cold, hungry, trembling after the roughness of travel, and with it all, a sickness it never knew before – that of loneliness.

FAR FROM HOME and playmates, and the world it has known, it peers out of the crate with frightened yet trusting eyes.

IT LOOKS ABOUT only to be disappointed for it had fancied dimly in its baby mind, that in some way, at the end of the journey, mother and the rest the family would be there to welcome it with a pretended sniff of curiosity and then would resume the customary play.

THE PAT OF a hand, a saucer of milk, a few softly spoken words, and almost a miracle transpires.

THE TAIL WAGS. The eyes become less drawn; they look up at you with a sort of soulful pleading. The legs wobble a bit, then walk.

THE CRATE, THE trembling and the unfriendly world are forgotten. The pup begins to explore the new home, every crack and corner – and ten days later, owns the house and everything in it, including yourself.

In Praise of the Female

NOTWITHSTANDING that prejudice often prefers her brother, the female dog has all the virtues of her species and fewer of the vices. Indeed it may be said that she excels the male in most of the good qualities which have endeared the dog to us as man's best friend.

IN A DOG we demand companionship, watchful guarding and usefulness as the occasion requires. These the female gives in greater measure and more gracefully than does the male.

HER COMPANIONSHIP is mellowed with a devotion more steadfast and gentle, ever given with the subtle charm of her sex.

SHE IS A keener watcher, feels a more constant sense of duty, and with motherly suspicion, discriminates more carefully between friend of the family and the stranger.

THE HOUSEWIFE has less trouble with conduct, fewer pieces of bric-a-brac to mend, and less sweeping to do.

HER GOOD manners are evident in the finesse with which she eats, in contrast to the male's greedy gulping.

IF HOUSEBREAKING can be regarded as a nasty task, choose the female-she is cleaner in the home, does her duties less frequently, and outdoors surely does them more modestly and over smaller area.

THE FEMALE is a homebody, jealous of the family possessions, whereas her brother may incline to be the tramp. The guilt of digging up a neighbour's flowers usually must be placed upon the roaming male.

THE FEMALE is less presumptuous unless it be with children; in them she assumes a motherly interest. She senses danger more quickly. The extra attention she pays to the baby of the household reveals an instinctive solicitude for the weak and helpless.

TRAINERS PREFER the female for she learns more quickly and keeps her mind on the task at hand. Her conscience is more sensitive to disobedience. On game in the field, she is fully as keen and successful.

WHEREAS THE male is in season all the year, the female comes into heat only twice a year and then for a scarce twenty days; she asks only that she be kept at home or, if outdoors, on a lead, during these brief periods.

IN NOTHING ELSE is the prejudice against the female dog (let us not hesitate to call her openly by the ancient and honourable name of bitch) so evident and unfair as with regard to her heat. When she has matured and in turn is ready to repeat the divine mystery of birth, she is shunned, almost cursed as though her sex were a plague, as though she should be punished for her sex and for the creative duties Nature has decreed for all of her sex in all species of animal life.

IN PUREBRED breeding, the female is just as important (and not a few authorities of heredity declare her more dominant) as the stud male; her pedigree is to be studied just as carefully.

FURTHER SHE has the advantage of motherhood; it is she who carries the allotment of coming life. She can be mated and thereby add her bit to the family's income through presenting her owner with duplicates of herself to carry on in other homes.

LOGICALLY INDEED the female is to be preferred to the male, and the prospective purchaser of a puppy well can place the advantage with her in making his choice.

MISS L. M. HIGNETT'S LOSTOCK LODESTAR.

Photograph by Hignett and Son, Lostock.

DIFFERENCES IN DOGS

Ay, in the catalogue ye go for men;
As hounds, and greyhounds, mongrels, spaniels, curs,
Shoughs, water-rugs, and demi-wolves are clepped
All by the name of dogs: the valued file
Distinguishes the swift, the slow, the subtle,
The housekeeper, the hunter, every one
According to the gift which bounteous nature
Hath in him closed; whereby he does receive
Particular addition from the bill
That writes them all alike: and so of men.

- SHAKESPEARE

THE DOG IN THE MANGER

An envious Dog that Brooding lay,
Upon a Crop Replete with Hay,
Snarls at the Ox that thither came,
An eager appetite to tame.
And forced him back, incensed, whereat
He on the Dog invokes this Fate:-
May the Just Gods so punish thee,
As thy Rude Spleen hath injured me,
Who Does prohibit me the meat,
Whereon they Self disdains to eat.

- APHRA BEHN (AESOP)

Why Own a Dog

THAT you may not forget how to play as exemplified by the dog who carries his puppy heart on through into the graying muzzle.

THAT you may have for your home and possessions an alert burglar alarm and a policeman who never sleeps.

THAT you may be reminded daily and with resultant humility that you and the animal kingdom are of one and the same group in the scheme of creation.

THAT you may live above petty selfishness through obligating yourself for the welfare of one who depends implicitly upon you and never complains if you are derelict.

THAT you may forget the worries of the day and the strain of its routine as arriving home, you are greeted with unfeigned delight by one whose heart is filled only with thought of you and whose existence, he believes, cannot go on apart from yours.

THAT you may find surcease from being bored through observing the dog's freshness in doing the customary little things, his curiosity over the flutter of a leaf to the ground, and his discovery of new delights along old paths.

THAT your children, growing up with a dog, may see a daily living sermon on kindness, obligation to others and the necessity for obedience, and that later they can translate these qualities into good citizenship.

THAT you may learn from your servant the dog to live with faith in fellowmen, with a readiness to forgive, and above all, with an unselfishness which may not be logical but is divinely refreshing.

THAT by your dog's contagious example, you may live each day to its fullness, be always ready for new adventure, and find zest in common and uncommon things alike.

THAT all these things may come to pass.

GET A DOG

OWN A DOG

AND BE OWNED BY A DOG.

Breeder's Code

1. I will study the bitch as well as the sire.
2. I will study grandparents rather than parents.
3. I will not pay attention to breeding superstitions.
4. I will interpret a pedigree by breeding facts and dominance rather than names and titles.
5. I will keep full breeding records and draw conclusions accordingly.
6. I will put away culls, weaklings and the deformed shortly after birth.
7. I will not breed, sell or give away a shy or excessively nervous dog.
8. I will judge a stud by his offspring even to the third generation.
9. I will honour most the bred-by-exhibitor dog.
10. I will give preference to breeding specimens of good temperament and strong nerves.
11. I will have patience to try again and again, and will not be discouraged by litters which are disappointments.
12. I will be led on constantly by the seductive dream of one day producing the perfect dog of my breed, and if another breeder forges ahead of me, I shall envy but also praise him.

The Dogist's Code

(Note – Henry L. Mencken in his Dictionary of American Language Vol. II., credits the author Will Judy with the origin of the word dogist.)

I. Colour all your work with a deep love for all dogs.

II. Be sympathetic counsellor to the novice for you yourself once knew as little as he.

III. Beware of him who is quick to find fault for likely you will be his target in time.

IV. Say nothing rather than out of malice, speak ill of another kennel or breed.

V. Seek business on your own merit rather than by taking it away from a competitor.

VI. Envy the competitor who forges ahead of you, but praise him also.

VII. Win with a smile of course, but to lose with a smile lessens the defeat and requires greater sportsmanship.

VIII. When you lose, resolve to come back to win at a later time.

IX. Show in yourself the same sportsmanship you demand of others.

X. Be the god-on-earth and all-wise master your dogs think you are.

THE DOG AND THE SHADOW

The Dog who with his prey the River swam
Saw his own laden Image in the stream.
The wishing Cur grown covetous of all,
To catch the Shadow lets the Substance fall.
                              - APHRA BEHN (AESOP)

THE DOGS OF NILE

Like the dogs of Nile be wise;
Who, taught by instinct how to shun
The crocodile, that lucking lies,
Run as they drink, and drink and run.
                              - SWIFT

WELCOMING THE DAWN

At morning's call
The small-voiced pug-dog welcomes in the sun,
And flea-bit mongrels, wakening one by one,
Give answer all.
                              - HOLMES

OLD-FASHIONED BLACK-AND-TAN TERRIERS (1881).

The Spirit of Sportsmanship
(A word of counsel to exhibitors at dog shows)

Dog shows are fascinating, thrilling, interesting. The afford opportunity for social contacts, for friendly gatherings, for sportsmen to gather from all sections of America. To win a blue or even the second red in strong competition gives deep pleasure.

The dogs themselves receive the best of care; in truth, most of them enjoy going away from the kennels to be posed in the show ring.

A dog may win against another mostly because he presents his good points to better advantage before the judge; he is "on his toes," properly posed for his particular breed. At tomorrow's show he may lose to the same dog.

If you have what you consider a typy specimen, enter him at one or more dog shows to get an official opinion through a licensed judge.

The placing of your dog at one show is only one man's opinion of your dog-the judge's, and on that particular day, it is official for that show. But the next show, another judge, liking your type of dog, and under different competition, may place your dog first. Few good dogs go through to the title without losing perhaps two of every five times.

One dog show does not make or break a dog. Some great winners were defeated at their first show.

Of course, you have the best dog in the world, until you meet another dog owner, and he will tell you that he has the best dog in the world. Both of you will be mostly right.

"Ten Commandments" for the Dog Owner

I. Give your dog a monthly physical examination: check his skin for possible irritation; "smell" the inside of his ears for possible canker infection. Every six months have his toe nails cut and teeth cleaned.

II. On snowy, rainy, slushy days, have a large, rough, absorbent towel just inside the door, within reach. Use it vigorously to clean, wipe, and dry the dog down to the skin-especially between the toes-when he comes back from his romp outdoors.

III. When you have guests in the house, make certain the dog does not paw the ladies' stockings; does not leap on the guests; does not make a nuisance of himself in any way.

IV. At least every two days, brush the dog's coat thoroughly – brush tenderly around ears and head. Make certain the bristles of the brush reach down to the skin in order to remove dandruff and other impurities.

V. Train your dog so that he knows his place in the house. It is never in the dining room while you are eating; never sleeping against the radiator, nor at top or bottom of stairways, nor in hallways. Have a definite place designated for him where to eat and sleep.

VI.	Regard your dog as a dog and not as half-human; no "baby talk," no coddling.
VII.	Do not wait until it is too late to take your dog to the veterinarian. Both the dog and the doctor want to live.
VIII.	Have regard for your neighbours and their rights and wishes by keeping your dog under control so that he does not damage their lawns or cause them annoyance.
IX.	Do not permit your dog to become a public nuisance or cause unsanitary conditions.
X.	Do not be unkind to your dog by overfeeding him so that he becomes lazy, unwatchful, clumsy, and ill.

THE UNDER DOG

I know that the world, the great big world,
Will never a moment stop
To see which dog may be in the fault,
But will shout for the dog on top.
But for me, I shall never pause to ask
Which dog may be in the right,
For my heart will beat, while it beats at all,
For the underdog in the fight.

- ANONYMOUS

BEAU'S REPLY

Sir, when I flew to seize the bird
In spite of your command,
A louder voice than yours I heard,
And harder to withstand.

You cried – forbear – but in my breast
A mightier cried – proceed –
'Twas nature, sir, whose strong behest
Impelled me to the deed.

Yet much as nature I respect,
I ventured once to break
(As you perhaps may recollect)
Her precept for your sake;

And when your linnet on a day,
Passing his prison door,
Had fluttered all his strength away,
And panting pressed the floor,

Well knowing him a sacred thing,
Not destined to my tooth,
I only kissed his ruffled wing,
And licked the feathers smooth.

Let my obedience then excuse
My disobedience now,
Nor some reproot yourself refuse
From your aggrieved Bow-wow:

If killing birds be such a crime
(Which I can hardly see),
What think you, sir, of killing time
With verse addressed to me?

- COWPER

A Dog's Prayer for His Master

O LORD OF HUMANS, make my master faithful to his fellowmen as I am to him. Grant that he may be devoted to his friends and family as I am to him.

MAY HE BE openfaced and undeceptive as I am; may he be true to trust reposed in him as I am to his.

GIVE HIM a face cheerful like unto my wagging tail. Give him a spirit of gratitude like unto my licking tongue.

FILL HIM WITH patience like unto mine that awaits his footsteps uncomplainingly for hours. Fill him with my watchfulness, my courage, and my readiness to sacrifice comfort or life itself.

KEEP HIM always young in heart and crowded with the spirit of play, even as I.

MAKE HIM as good a man as I am dog. Make him worthy of me, his dog.

Photo by M. & A. Austin, St. Albans.]

BANTAM.

STILL 'MAN'S BEST FRIEND'

Bringing up a puppy to doghood is an achievement and also a practical course in teaching. One becomes a master of animal psychology and an expert in pedagogy. Even the bachelor and spinster dog owners go through the similar duties of a parent.

But the work and the worry, the cleaning up after the puppy, the reprimands and the disappointments – all are worth while and are well repaid by the dog as he develops into an appreciative, loyal, obedient, faithful member of the household.

A little soft warm bundle of fur which came into your home greatly frightened, biologically one of the beasts of the field, has almost bridged the wide gap between the human race and the animal kingdom. He has come out of the fields and forests of his ancestors to live by your side in the midst of modern civilization; and he makes the adjustment splendidly.

There is no other instance of such great progress from one stage to another as that of the dog, which adjusts himself to all the needs and desires of man. He comes from savagery to civilization within the short period of twelve months and indeed represents man's greatest achievement over the animal kingdom.

Give that four-footed member of your family the consideration and care to which you are obligated; and when in old age he moves slowly, his eyes water, and he dreams of puppyhood days, his passing on will be that of a loved and lovable member of the family whose soul never knew dishonesty and deceit.

THE MIRACLE OF MATING AND BIRTH

The work of dog breeding has these progressive steps – choice of parents, the mating, the period of in whelp or pregnancy of the dam or bitch, the whelping of the litter of puppies, nursing and care of puppies for the first eight weeks, care, development and supervision of the poppies after eight weeks.

But the most interesting, most fascinating of the six steps is the delivery or whelping of the puppies out of the mother's womb. Something new comes into the world of conscious being; life appears for the first time to the outside world; the miracle of mating and birth is being climaxed. The spark of being bursts into the full flame of life – and the dog breeder therefore, if he be a true devotee of the sport of breeding, never fails to enjoy anew each time the thrill of ushering a new litter into the world of dogs and humans.

THE SIXTEEN PRINCIPLES OF DOG PEDAGOGY

1. All dog training must be founded upon "educating" the dog, that is, first drawing out of him and developing his instincts, and secondly, accidental and acquired abilities.
2. Situations and contacts must be interpreted entirely from the dog's, not the human's reactions and abilities.

3. The dog is not to be fooled. He has a sense of humiliation and of pride. If he has been taught to do a certain act, do not give him the command and then trifle with him. At all times let him see what you are doing.

4. Success must be at the completion of an act of training. The dog is to understand that at the end a certain thing will take place; for instance, if he is trailing, he must find the object trailed. Always he is to understand that when you say certain things, he is to do certain things, there must not be any break in this seeming cause and effect.

5. Commands should be given consistently in the same words and with the same tone of voice and speed of speaking.

6. Do not punish the dog for failures to obey unless you are certain that he understood fully what you commanded.

7. Give the dog a moment's time for carrying out your command. To demand instant obedience often is to confuse the dog.

8. Anticipate the dog's actions. Think ahead of him. Give your command not to step over a boundary line before he reaches the line.

9. If the dog does one step wrongly, do not repeat this step but begin again at the beginning for the dog must be taught to consider only successful acts in their entirety.

10. The dog has a single-track mind. Teach one specific thing at a time. This does not mean that

a training period can not include a half-dozen different tasks.

11. Reward should follow after every act done properly. Punishment should follow after every disobedience or failure.

12. Reward or punishment should follow quickly after the act. To punish a dog at any time other than instantly after the wrong act, is cruelty rather that part of training, for the dog, particularly a puppy, does not connect the punishment with the act.

13. Instruction should not be too long, as a dog, especially one under eight months, tires easily. An hour twice daily is sufficient length of time for special training work.

14. Try to locate each activity and command at or near the same location. If you call "brush," it should be at or near the place you groom the dog. This rule is based upon the law of association of ideas.

15. Do not lose your temper while training the dog. If you do, he loses some of his respect for you.

16. Have patience. The dog is not a human being. He probably is more successful as a dog than you are as a human being. His pleading liquid eyes and his wagging tail tell that he wants to do what you would have him do but that you are not as intelligent as he, else you would tell him in his language what you wish to say to him.

EXTRACT

A swirl of gold-and-white and gray and black, -
Rackety, vibrant, glad with life's hot zest, -
Sunnybank collies, gaily surging pack, -
These are my chums; the chums that love me best.

Not chums alone, but courtiers, zealots, too,-
Clean-white of soul, too wise for fraud or sham;
Yet senseless in their worship ever new.
These are the friendly folk whose god I am.

A blatant, foolish, stumbling, purblind god,-
A pinchbeck idol, clogged with feet of clay!
Yet, eager at my lightest word or nod,
They crave but leave to follow and obey.

We humans are so slow to understand!
Swift in our wrath, deaf to the justice-plea,
Meting out punishment with lavish hand!
What, but a dog, would serve such gods as we?

Heaven gave them souls, I'm sure; but dulled the brain,
Les they should sadden at so brief a span
Of heedless, honest life as they sustain;
Or doubt the godhead of their master, Man.

Today a pup; tomorrow at life's prime;
Then old and fragile; -dead at fourteen years.
At best a meagre little inch of time.
Oblivion then, sans mourners, memories, tears!

Service that asks no price; forgiveness free
For injury or for injustice hard.
Stanch friendship, wanting neither thanks nor fee
Save privilege to worship and to guard:-

That is their creed. They know no shrewder way
To travel through their hour of lifetime here.
Would Man but deign to serve his God as they,
Millennium must dawn within the year.

                    - ALBERT PAYSON TERHUNE

GOOD DOGS

False friends, who love our gladsome hours,
In darksome days may flee;
But till our dogs deserters prove,
We cannot friendless be.

They love us still, through good and ill,
Through bright and stormy days;
And only ask, for service true,
One word of kindly praise.

For our dear sakes to shield and save,
Both fire and flood they brave;
They watch beside our dying-beds,
And mourn us at the grave.

The hero of a hundred fights
Has not his laurels won
By nobler deeds of courage high,
Than our good dogs have done!

                    - MRS. SURR

CH. COQUETTE.

DOGS CAN BE TOUGHIES

The English press reports that a dog named Rex had been given up as dead on account of being buried in the debris of his master's home, that of W. J. Humphries, Birmingham, when an enemy bomb struck the house.

Six weeks later, as reported in the English Weekly Dog World: "Mr Humphries returned to the house to salvage what he could of his goods, and while searching among the wreckage, heard a whimper. With his bare hands Mr. Humphries began to dig and he found Rex lying helpless under the twisted remains of a bed. Rex could not stand for three days, but with careful attention he is recovering. It is hoped that he will pull through after his terrible experience."

The Editor has been criticized severely for stating in his various books that many dog owners are cruel to their dogs through the mistaken kindness of overfeeding them. Few dogs die of starvation; most dogs die indirectly through the contrary, being overfed and consequently acquiring digestive ills, which in turn lead on to vital illness.

THE DOG AS A WORD STUDY IN
INTERNATIONAL ORTHOGRAPHY

The word dog in other languages is an interesting study
of orthography.
Chinese – kou.
Danish, German, Norwegien – hund
French – chien
Hebrew – keleb
Irish – cu
Italian – cane
Japanese – inu
Belgian , Dutch – hond
Polish – pies
Russian – sobaka
Spanish – perro
Swedish – hundar
Czech – pes
Hungarian – kutya
Welsh – ki
Lithuanian – suo

REVENGE

Lo, when two dogs are fighting in the streets,
With a third dog one of the two dogs meets;
With angry teeth he bites him to the bone,
and this dog smarts for what that dog has done.
FIELDING

TED

I have a little brindle dog,
Seal-brown from tail to head.
His name I guess is Theodore,
But I just call him Ted.

He's only eight months old to-day
I guess he's just a pup;
Pa says he won't be larger
When he is all grown up.

He plays around about the house,
As good as he can be,
He don't seem like a little dog,
He's just like folks to me.

And when it is my bed-time,
Ma opens up the bed;
Then I nestle down real cozy
And just make room for Ted

And oh, how nice we cuddle!
He doesn't fuss or bit,
Just nestles closely up to me
And lays there still all night.

We love each other dearly,
My little Ted and me.
We're just good chums together,
And always hope to be.

Why the World Likes Dogs

THE MOST UNSELFISH living thing in the world is your dog. If you are in danger, your dog needs only to hear your cry of distress to rush to your aid, without thought of his own life, fearless of guns and enemies.

THE MOST PATIENT thing in the world is your dog, waiting for hours at the door to hear the sound of your footsteps, never complaining however late you may be.

THE MOST GRATEFUL thing in the world is your dog. Whatever you give him, whatever you do for him, he never is guilty of ingratitude. A pat of the hand, a soft-spoken word from you are golden pay. To him you are the most powerful personage in the world and beyond censure; you are your dog's god; you can do no wrong.

THE MOST FRIENDLY thing in the world is your dog. Of all the animal kingdom, he alone serves man without whip, without compulsion, glad to be by the side of his master wherever he may be, whatever he may do, and sad in heart when his master is away.

THE MOST FORGIVING thing in the world is your dog. The one virtue most humans lack is that of forgiveness. But your dog carries no grudge and no spite. Punish him even underservedly, and he comes to you, nudges his moist nose against your hand, lookds up at you with pleading eyes, and wags his tail hesitatingly as though to say, "Oh, come on, let's be pals again."

THE MOST LOYAL thing in the world is your dog. Whether you come home from Congress or from jail, whether you have lost your fortune or made a million, whether you return dressed in fashion's splendour or in wretched rags, whether you have been hailed hero or condemned as criminal, your dog is waiting for you with a welcoming bark of delight, a wagging tail and a heart that knows no guile.

The world likes dogs because dogs are nearest to moral perfection of all living things.

No Room in Heaven for Dogs

(An answer by the editor of Dog World to a letter from a 12-year old school boy)

I am sorry that your Sunday School teacher told you "there is no room in heaven for dogs." I can understand that this statement has disturbed you considerable.

Heaven is a big place because heaven is God and God stretches from the sun to the moon, to the stars, and back to earth.

Heaven must be a big place to hold all the good people who have died in the many years since the world began. As angels have wings, heaven must give them plenty of space in which to spread these wings and fly from one shifting cloud to another.

The millions upon millions of folks who have owned dogs and gone on to their heavenly home, surely would feel lonely without their dogs. And as there is no loneliness in heaven, God has made provision for man's best friend to dwell therein. We are certain of this, for it was God who named the dog by spelling His own name backwards.

Yes, heaven is a big place, with lots of shady spots, long lanes banked with flowers, fountains bubbling up out of the earth, good little rabbits munching on golden carrots, and by their side good dogs, big and little, dozing in the pure sunshine of celestial spaces.

It would be surprisingly strange, were there no dogs in heaven, for I believe that Christ had a little dog which followed him back and forth from Nazareth to Judea, through the streets of Jerusalem, and cuddled trustingly in the boat when He crossed the stormy sea of Galilee.

It seems to me I can see, on that tragic afternoon on Calvary, as Christ cried out "Why has Though forsaken me?", a little dog whining vainly at the foot of the cross to lick His bleeding hands. I believe that today this same little dog can be no other place than in heaven with Christ his master, lying contentedly at the foot of the throne of God.

I am sorry indeed that someone gave you the misinformation that "there is no room in heaven for dogs."

Ch. Glenartney Laddie.

WE ARE VICARS OF GOD

The Almighty created humans with the possibilities lurking within themselves of becoming godlike, approaching even to the Creator himself.

All other living things of the animal kingdom are termed the dumb creation or the lower animals. This term of inferiority is man-made and may not be in accord with the Creator's design of importance.

In primeval days the animals of the field and forest were on more nearly equal terms with the human animals. In this present age, with its myriads of inventions and machines, man has adjusted himself but the lower animals still retain mostly the capabilities of the primeval days, not having developed a language and a set of fingers and thumbs.

Therefore, the obligation is upon us to do for these living things that which they cannot do for themselves – to avoid unnecessary pain and suffering, to have opportunity to live their lives naturally and rear their young safely and to have the means of fulfilling their varying purposes in the plan of creation.

Surely we are only being appreciative of our status in the celestial scheme of things when we show consideration to all other living things and thereby, as it were, stand in the stead of the Creator.

It is for man, the allegedly superior animal, to show this superiority in kindness rather than force, in sympathetic understanding rather than brutal disregard.

We are vicars of God in this respect. Truly there is no surer way for the human soul to climb the heights than to have a constant, kindly regard for those considered as not having a soul or at best, an inferior one.

The Dog Issues 'His' Ten Commandments

1. Be sure you know more than I do before you attempt to teach and train me.
2. Look at my problems or any of your efforts to train me through my eyes and mind.
3. Don't become impatient with me until after you are certain I understand fully what you want me to do. Get your ideas across to me. Remember-I don't speak with words.
4. Don't lose your temper; it only makes you look weak and ridiculous to us dogs.
5. Make sure the water in my drinking pan is not stale, dust-filled, or unclean. Don't put anything in my drinking dish except clean, pure water.
6. I haven't hands for using brush and comb; so please groom me at least once every two days, else don't complain about canine body odour.

7.   If I bark when I hear strange sounds, don't
        reprimand me too quickly. It is not easy for
        me to tell who is friendly and who is intent
        upon doing harm.
8.   Give me a bit of notice when you approach
        me, especially if I am sleeping, or have my
        back turned.
9.   On the street, keep tab on me, especially if I
        spy another dog across the street. Don't let me
        leave the curb.
10.   Be proud of me as I am of you. And please, if I
        am ill, don't wait too long before you take me
        to my favourite veterinarian.

A PLEASING KIND OF INSANITY

That otherwise good people should travel the detour of a
hobby and become abnormally zealous therein, at times
to the detriment of their calling, is well known; but
perhaps, it is not too well known that in this regard,
indeed the most temperamental and seemingly fanatical
are the dog breeders, the exhibitors at dog shows; and in
general, all dog fanciers. Age is immaterial; the neophytes
are as temperamental and high-strung as the old-timers.

They appear to be abnormal; they resent criticism; they
extol their own dogs as the most desirable of all. Each
one seeks the mirage of perfection in physical type,
knowing full well that the perfect canine never exists –
and so they learn to their disillusionment in the show

ring time after time; but such defeats do not dampen their ardour through the years.

They carry on furiously and at times vociferously. They may even neglect their own money-making calling or permit it to suffer. They are strange folk; they argue with and against one another; they become mad competitors; yet in an instant, they shake hands, embrace each other and the losers congratulate the victor.

Indeed here is strange company! On the whole they are warm-hearted people; the subject of their hobby is a living, understanding thing; they deal in life itself; their obsession is not with ordinary live stock but with an animal which is said to come nearest to man in mental capabilities – namely, the dog, 'man's best friend,' so-called.

Yet notwithstanding all these things, we consider the dog people as warm-hearted and likeable folks tainted with a pleasing kind of insanity.

Pity the Sick Dog

What is ahead for the sick animal in the fields? We all have seen a bird perched solemnly without motion for hours. Likely this bird is in the last stages of a disease which soon will drop it to the ground.

Just so with the old animal, the sick animal in the forest, and the dog that cannot protect itself against other dogs, that cannot go out and forage for its own food, where it must match cleverness and strength against that of its prey. Instead, it must lie quietly awaiting the end of life.

Pity the old dog, the sick dog, the crippled dog in the wilds!

"Faithful Barking Ghost"

"But in some canine Paradise
    Your wraith, I know, rebukes the moon.
And quarters every plain and hill,
    Seeking its master. As for me
    This prayer at least the gods fulfil
That when I pass the flood and see
Old Charon by Stygian coast
    Take toll of the shades who land,
Your little, faithful barking ghost
    May leap to lick my phantom hand!"
                              -St. John Lucas

THE DIFFERENCE

My dog! The difference between thee and me
Knows only our Creator – only he
Can number the degrees in being's scale
Between th'Instinctive lamp, ne'er known to fail,
And that less steady light, of brighter ray,
The soul which animates thy master's clay;
And he alone can tell by what fond tie
My look thy life, my death thy sign to die.

No, when that feeling quits thy glazing eye
'Twill live in some blest world beyond the sky.
                                    - ANONYMOUS

LITTLE LOST PUP

He was lost! – Not a shade of doubt of that;
For he never barked at a slinking cat,
But stood in the square where the wind blew raw,
With a drooping ear, and a trembling paw,
And a mournful look in his pleading eye,
And a plaintive sniff at the passer-by
That begged as plain as a tongue could sue,
"Oh, Mister, please may I follow you?"
A lorn, wee waif of a tawny brown
Adrift in the roar of a heedless town.
Oh, the saddest of sights in a world of sin
Is a little lost pup with his tail tucked in"

Well, he won my heart (for I set great store
On my own red Bute, who is here no more)
So I whistled clear, and he trotted up,
And who so glad as that small lost pup?

Now he shares my board, and he owns my bed,
And he fairly shouts when he hears my tread.
Then if things go wrong, as they sometimes do,
And the world is cold, and I'm feeling blue,
He asserts his right to assuage my woes
With a war, red tongue and a nice, cold nose.
And a silky head on my arm or knee,
And a paw as soft as a paw can be.

When we rove the woods for a league about
He's as full of pranks as a school let out;
For he romps and frisks like a three-months colt,
And he runs me down like a thunder-bolt.
Oh, the blithest of sights in the world so fair
Is a gay little pup with his tail in air!
                              - ANONYMOUS

MY DOG AND I

When living seems but little worth
And all things go awry,
I close the door, we journey forth –
My dog and I!

For books and pen we leave hehind,
But little careth he,
His one great joy in life is just
To be with me.

He notes by just one upward glance
My mental attitude,
As on we go past laughing stream
And singing wood.

The soft winds have a magic tough
That brings to care release,
The trees are vocal with delight,
The rivers sing of peace

How good it is to be alive!
Nature, the healer strong,
Has set each pulse with life athrill
And joy and song.

Discouragement! 'Twas but a name,
And all things that annoy,
Out in the lovely world of June
Life seemeth only joy!

And ere we reach the busy town,
Like birds my troubles fly,
We are two comrades glad of heart –
My dog and I!

                              - ALICE J. CLEATOR

BAGATELLE.

Lost Dog

Whatever the cause of the dog being away from its accustomed surroundings, away from the humans it regards as godlike and indispensable, the mental pain of the dog must be intense.

Who at one time or another has not seen a dog running strangely along the street, terror in its eyes, its movements indicating total bewilderment? If one tries to be kindly-disposed to the dog, to speak a soft word, to seek to pat the dog, it looks up with a ray of hope in its eyes, then as it realizes the person is not the one he seeks, the pang is sharper than ever and the dog rushes away, block after block, until – well, one wonders what will be the ending – death under grinding auto wheels, the remainder of the years in heartsick separation, or perhaps at last the happy ending – reunited with owners and family.

Let us be realistic. In most cases the lost dog is lost because of the owner's negligence, either accidental or habitual. Keep your dog under control, worry about him, don't permit him out of your sight – better still, in public places have him on lead.

The too friendly dog is a likely victim of being lost, of being enticed away. It is a fine line to draw especially for the dog, between being too friendly and being wisely aloof. Do not permit strangers to be too friendly with your dog. I know this is strange advice but I believe it is wise advice.

Dognappers are doing their work constantly – despicable humans who snatch a beloved dog away, then scan the papers for reward offer. Dog thieves of course always are to be feared – those who steal dogs for sale to unscrupulous dog shops, to other individuals, or to laboratories and medical school classes.

IF YOUR DOG IS LOST, SOUND THE NEWS EVERYWHERE.
Scour the neighbour hood promptly. Ask all neighbours whether they have seen your dog. Ads in newspapers of course are a necessity. Visit the dog pound and the local animal shelter. If school is in session, ask the principal to post a notice. Offer a reward to the children; they all become zealous detectives.

Do not give up hope. Dogs have returned or been returned six months to a year after disappearance.

You should have an identification tag on the dog's collar – with phone number. Be able to describe your dog precisely for colour, makings, habits, size, etc. Always mention call name of dog.

Best of all, alert yourself and family before the dog has disappeared. A trained dog, properly controlled, is less apt to stray away and less apt to permit itself to be picked up.

The Faith of a Dog

I've hunted the woodland and hill,
    And "pointed" the quail in my day,
I could freeze as rigid and still
    As a stone – when scent blew my way.
I recall the time you lost me
    And I "pointed" the long hours through –
Though the night was too dark to see,
    You came, as I knew you would do.
You gave me a pat in the darkness
    And your voice was roughened and gruff –
But I knew by that one caress
    That you understood well enough.
I'm just a dog but I love you,
    And though I am stiffened and old –
My heart is as brave and as true,
    My spirit still dauntless and bold.
I know that my hunting is done
    I no longer gambol and bark –
But this one desire I have won,
    Your hand on my head – in the dark!

MARGARET NICKERSON MARTIN
(blind poet)

Photo by S. J. Jarvis, Ottawa, Ont.
TOPSY

WALKDEN DUKE

CH DAISY

CH. BROOMFIELD SULTAN

CH. MEERSBROOK MAIDEN

CH. PERFECTO

Photo by S. O'Connor Ottawa, Ont.
PEGGIE

CH. RAZZLE

Observations of "Jay" upon the Five Great Wags. The Best Friends of Children and Men.

Dogs are the closest friends of children and men. Children come first for a dog's love, because of their understanding, and because dogs and children can but poorly tell of all that is in their hearts. Dogs have no words, and children but few.

The Boy has asked me to tell of some adventure in my life. But when I come to put the words down, I seem to think of no adventure which I care to speak of; for I am full of more serious matters. Besides, to tell of any of my great doings would take too much time. I do not want you to think that my life has been without strange and wonderful doings; that is not so – for it is crowded every day with many things worth telling. But I feel more like first letting you know of a dog's nature – his thoughts, pleasures, and feelings. I will do this; and some day I will speak of my "Great Fight with Uglymug," or my "Long Watch at the Door," or "How I Saved Boy," or "The Terrible Cat-Killing." (I was *blood wild* when I got into the last; so my good side shames me now.) These are a few of many adventures I have had. If the children really want me to, I will tell of any one, or all, some time.

Today I hear the wind blowing from the dear south into the tree-tops, the flies are making a singing sound, the sun is hot in spots on the ground, and many heavy smells come to my nose, each on with tempting colours. I sniff and sniff, and wish to shake myself hard and sharp, to drop the laziness off me, and go to seek adventures, not to tell of them. Today is a great tail-wagging time; so I must tell of the pleasure I have in it, and it may be when I get started on that subject I will speak of nothing else. I have a splendid tail for wagging purposes, and it is a constant joy and satisfaction to me.

First in the order of good wagging is the "Wag of deep love" for your Boy or Man friend. Of course, it is full of differences, according to the time of place, or Dog, but in the main it is the same, and Love is Love wherever the place be. So the wag is slow and sure from side to side and half-way in the air, never tight or rigid; it goes with ears neither back nor forward too far, and the eye-light is soft and appealing.

Second comes the "Great joy wag." This is begun with yaps, barks, whines away down in the throat, then jumps, runs, and licking of the hands, with violent wags every which way, all at once and well mixed up together. When you get a little settled down and sure the Master is there, well, happy, and loving you, you trot behind and smell his heel once in a while, or lick his hand to make him look at you. Then the last of the "joy wag" is to twist your body into a crook, as crooked as possible, and wag sidewise, stiff, and with little contented jerks. This is the dearest wag of all; a good dog loves it most, though it may not be so important as "deep love." It is felt all over the body and into the heart (dogs with bad dispositions cannot wag this way).

Third is the "Wag of alertness," and is used on many different occasions, but always when the mind is awake, keen, and watchful. This wag is somewhat hard to describe; for it is purely "dog," and needs understanding more than words to show what it means; but you can easily tell it, and know right well what it is. The wag may be seen when I am at a rat-hole, and is wagged to show that I know you are there and that I love you, but I do not want to be disturbed, or when I want to get after Jerry the cat, but don't dare, or when I see a stranger dog, that may be either friend or foe. To do this wag properly you must draw your tail up as high as possible, keeping it very stiff, then wag short and sharp, being careful to have no more on one side than the other; for it should become one-sided, you would lose grip of yourself, and appear undignified as well. The ears should be thrust sharply forward and never budged until things are settled or stiffness is no longer necessary.

Fourth – the "Dream wag." This one may not seem very important in the way of general wags, nor am I sure it should be fourth on the list, but it is to me very strange and interesting, leaving a great impression on my awakened mind. I carry a misty memory of it about with me when I am not very busy and on moonlight nights. There may be natural reasons for the "dream wag," – as, for instance, a fly on the ear where the hair is thin, too much heat from the fire, or a flea in the middle of your back, - but *I* think it is caused by going into another world, where wags change their methods and dogs speak with men's words. The Boy says my "dream wag" is queer and makes him afraid, and that I give hitchy jerks at the very end of my tail seven times, my jaws jerk and twitch, and my whine sounds far off in a very distant dog. I sometimes remember my dream; it is mixed –

pain, pleasure, and strangeness. I could tell you a dog-dream if I had time.

Fifth – Next comes the "Scratch wag." I might have left this one out, for some people will think it is not important; but it has always seemed to me that to get a pleasure without hurting anyone else or injuring yourself was perfectly right, and scratching your back hurts no one and gives you great happiness. The wag that goes along with this is almost any wag you care to make use of, varied in vigour according to the goodness or poorness of the scratching. I find that under the barn one can enjoy a fine continuous scratch in peace and quiet, if only the floor is neither too high nor too low and there are no green-eyed cats looking on. Then, there is a pleasant mystery and uncertainty about it all, and considerable satisfaction in knowing that no one sees how much fun you are having, or thinks you are a weak character because your wags are so mixed up with whines, growls, and throaty barks.

All that I have told you has been of the happy side of a dog's life, - that is, so far as his tail is concerned, - and I am loath to say anything of the *sixth* wag, which expresses all sorrow. But it may be that my words will sink deep into the heard of some boy, - so deep that he will never stand still unrebelling, when he sees a "fear wag." A dog's joy is blotted out by cruelty and abuse, and he is never the same again, having once been "cowed." Think of a *tail* wagging when he crawls along on his belly, twisting and squirming in trembling terror, with eyes full of fear and prayer! What would a smile upon your lips be, if terror and panic filled your heart, and your body drew together to receive a blow? When I see that sight I get the *blood fury*, and fear that some day I shall do terrible things to the coward of cowards, the low Man, who uses his mind and strength to flood a dumb creature's life with fear, and makes a tail to wag in cringing terror, when it should only be wagged for love, joy, and keen thinking.

I have now told you of the *five great waggings*, and the one wag of fear, which should not be counted, but still is sometimes seen. I have told of nothing else but wags, because wagging is of first importance. Of course, the tail is used in different ways by different dogs (but look out for the dog that never wags his tail, or has not tail). Wags and smiles make the heart kind. Barks, growls, yelps, and whines express a great deal, but I would give them all up rather than the "five waggings."

If the children want to know more about a dog's life, why he howls at the moon, growls in his sleep, loves to chase cats, hates some people, loves children – or anything of dogs' knowledge about dogs – let them ask me. Now the sun is soft and warm, the flies sing with their wings, streaks of blue smell come out of the woods and over the fields. I shall go to see what I may find. Wag joyfully! Good bye! Wag joyfully! Good bye!

- MORGAN SHEPARD

"Now I Have a Friend"

I had many friends in my lifetime-
Some who would borrow my very last dime;
I went through life, earned what I spent
Paid what I owed, lost what I lent.
My partner in business ran off with my wife,
Then stole my child and ruined my life,
The big bank failed where I kept my dough,
My house burned down, I had no place to go.
They all quit me cold when I could not lend.
So I bought me a dog – now I have a friend.

ANONYMOUS

An Outcast in Hell
(or the Dog Poisoner)

During a lull in the Stygian flames
      A group of shades were exchanging names,
And telling of places that they had been
      With bits of gossip and tales of sin.
A lonely shade who was standing by
      Approached to speak; but without reply
Each wrapped himself in his ghostly shawl!
      Murderers, robbers and blackguards all
With a whispered word and averted stare
      Vanished and left him standing there.
"Who was he?" I asked as they turned and fled.
      "He poisoned his neighbour's dog," they said.

ANONYMOUS

MANCHESTER TERRIER.

BENHAM FOILER.　　　　　PLATE XXXV.

The Dog in the Library

So good you never knew that he was there
     Until you came upon him in a nook
Beside the small grey woman as she searched
     The well-known shelves for some yet unread
     book.
He waited patiently as she would thumb
     The leaves, and when she sauntered on he went
Pad-footed at her side, a little dog
     Brown-patched, clean-white, devoted and
     content.
Perhaps this dalliance bored him but he gave
     No hint of tedium-no whimpered sound,
No tapping paws, no straining at the leash.
     Only, at times when girls and boys would bound
Into the quiet place his eager eyes
     Would follow them about the library,
And when swift choice they made and ran to play,
     He seemed to watch their going wistfully.

ETHEL KING

THE BEST DOG

Yes, I went to see the bow-wows, and I looked at every
one,
Proud dogs of each breed and strain that's underneath
the sun;
But not one could compare with – you may hear it with
surprise –
A little yellow dog I know that never took a prize.

Not that they would have skipped him when they gave
the ribbons out,
Had they been a class to fit him – though his lineage is
in doubt.
No judge of dogs could e'er resist the honest, faithful
eyes
Of that plain little yellow dog that never took a prize.

Suppose he wasn't trained to hunt, and never killed a rat,
And isn't much on tricks or looks or birth – well, what
of that?
That might be said of lots of folks whom men call great
and wise,
As well as of that yellow dog that never took a prize.

It isn't what a dog can do, or what a dog may be,
That hits a man. It's simply this – does he believe in me?
And by that test I know there's not the compeer 'neath
the skies
Of that plain little yellow dog that never took a prize.

Oh, he's the finest little pup that ever wagged a tail,
And followed man with equal joy to Congress or to jail.

I'm going to start a special show – 'Twill beat the world
for size –
For faithful little yellow dogs, and each shall have a prize.

- ANONYMOUS

DOG LANGUAGE

Our Towser is the finest dog that ever wore a collar,
We wouldn't sell him – no, indeed – not even for a
dollar!
I understand his language now, 'cause honest, it appears
That dogs can talk, and say a lot, with just their tails and
ears.

When I come home from school he meets me with a
joyous bound,
And shakes that long tail sideways, down and up, and
round and round.
Pa says he's going to hang a rug beside the door to see
If Towser will not beat it while he's busy greeting me.

Then when he sees me get my hat, but thinks he cannot
go,
His ears get limp, his tail drops sown, and he just walks
off – slow;
Though if I say the magic words: "Well, Towser, want to
come?"
Why, say! You'd know he answered "Yes," although at
speech he's dumb.

- MARION HOVEY BRIGGS

The Story of a Great Literary Gem

The world around, Senator Vest's Eulogy of the Dog is read and admired. Many varying stories have been written about the actual event, but a careful search of archives reveals the following, which the author assures is authentic.

On the front of the Old Courthouse in Warrensburg, Mo., a two-and-a-half story brink structure, no longer used, a bronze tablet bears this inscription:

"Within these walls on Sept. 23, 1870, Senator George Graham Vest delivered his famous eulogy on the dog. He died Aug. 14, 1904, and was buried in Bellefontaine Cemetery, St. Louis."

Old Drum, a black and tan coonhound owned by Charles Burden, was enjoying one of his usual trailing jaunts through the woods when a neighbour "Lon" Hornsby, redheaded and stubborn, shot Old Drum. However, it is to be noted that Hornsby, a reputable farmer and livestock rancher, had suffered the loss of more than 100 of his sheep during the few months previous.

On the evening of Oct. 28, 1869, Hornsby asked his companion, Richard Ferguson, to shoot the dog, as they detected Old Drum nearby in the twilight.

Burden filed a suit before the Justice of the Peace in Madison Township but the jury at the trial Nov. 25, 1869, failed to reach a decision and the case was set for retrial on the following Dec. 23.

Public feeling ran high on one side or the other and the second trial was well attended by farmers, cattle raisers and hunters of the area. Here Burden was awarded $25. Hornsby, his neighbour, appealed to Johnson Country Court of Common Pleas. This new trial, in March, 1870, with two attorneys on each side, brought a verdict in favour of Hornsby.

Burden, in turn, asked for and won a new trial. This fourth trial became a public mass meeting with the crowds overflowing the capacity of the courthouse.

The wagering on the outcome of the trial was about even up to the point when George Graham Vest of Phillips and Vest of Sedalia, Mo., attorneys for Burden, arose for the final argument for their client — this on Sept. 23, 1870.

Vest spoke for only a few minutes. The jury cam back promptly and returned the verdict in favour of Burden and Old Drum — for $50, twice the amount sued for originally.

Nine attorneys in all were connected with the case. One of them was David Nation, no other than the husband of the famous Carrie Nation. Elliott became judge of the Court of Common Pleas of Johnson County.

T. T. Crittenden later was elected governor of Missouri. Cockrell was a senator from that state for 30 years and afterward became a member of the Interstate Commerce Commission. John F. Phillips was appointed a commissioner of the Supreme Court of Mo. George Graham Vest was U.S. Senator from Mo. For 24 years.

MANCHESTER TERRIER.

BESTWICK BEAUTY.

Senator Vest's Tribute to a Dog
THE TRIBUTE

THE BEST FRIEND a man has in the world may turn against him and become his enemy. His son or daughter that he has reared with loving care may prove ungrateful. Those who are nearest and dearest to us, those whom we trust with our happiness and our good name, may become traitors to their faith.

THE MONEY a man has he may lose. It flies away from him when he needs it most. A man's reputation may be sacrificed in a moment of ill-considered action. The people who are prone to fall on their knees to do us honour when success is with us, may be the first to throw stones of malice when failure settles its clouds upon our heads.

THE ONE absolutely unselfish friend that a man can have in this selfish world, the one that never deserts him, the one that never proves ungrateful or treacherous, is his dog.

A MAN'S DOG stands by him in prosperity and in poverty, in health and in sickness. He will sleep on the cold ground where the wintry winds blow and the snow drives fiercely if only he may be near his master's side. He will kiss the hand that has no food to offer, he will lick the sores and wounds that come in encounter with the roughness of the world. He guards the sleep of his pauper master as if he were a prince.

WHEN ALL other friends desert, he remains. When riches take wings and reputation falls to pieces, he is as constant in his love as the sun in its journey through the heavens.

IF MISFORTUNE drives the master forth an outcast in the world, friendless and homeless, the faithful dog asks no higher privilege than that of accompanying him to guard against danger, to fight against his enemies.

My Dog

Through glad days and sad days
    We two have clung together;
O'er rough roads and tough roads
    In every kind of weather.
Our square meals and spare meals
    Have both been shared together;
On warm nights and storm nights
    We've slept amongst the heather.
A fair friend, a rare friend
    Who never asks me whether
It's byways or highways
    Just so we are together.
          WM. H. RUMSEY

TRIBUTE TO DOG - 1200 A.D.

Nothing is more busy and wittier than a hound, for he hath more wit than other beasts.

And hounds know their own names, and love their masters, and defend the houses of their masters, and put themselves wilfully in peril of death for their masters, and run to take prey for their masters, and forsake not the dead bodies of their masters.

We have known that hounds fought for their lords against thieves, and were sore wounded, and that they kept away beasts and fowls from their masters' bodies dead. And that a hound compelled the slayer of his master with barking and biting to acknowledge his trespass and guilt.

The Power of the Dog

There is sorrow enough in the natural way
From men and women to fill our day;
But when we are certain of sorrow in store,
Why do we always arrange for more?
Brothers and sisters, I bid you beware
OF GIVING YOUR HEART TO A DOG TO TEAR!

We've sorrow enough in the natural way,
When it comes to burying Christian clay.
Our loves are not given, but only lent,
At compound interest at cent per cent.

Though it is not always the case, I believe,
That the longer we've kept 'em, the more we do grieve:
For, when debts are payable, right or wrong,
A short time loan is as bad as a long-
So why in Heaven (before we are there)
SHOULD WE GIVE OUR HEARTS TO A DOG TO
TEAR?

Buy a pup and your money will buy
Love unflinching that cannot lie-
Perfect passion and worship fed
By a kick in the ribs or a pat on the head.
Nevertheless, it is hardly fair
TO RISK YOUR HEART FOR A DOG TO TEAR

When the fourteen years that Nature permits
Are closing in asthma, or tumour, or fits,
And the vet's unspoken prescription runs
To lethal chambers or loaded guns,
Then you will find-it's your own affair,
BUT...YOU'VE GIVEN YOUR HEART TO A DOG
TO TEAR.

When the body that lived at your single will,
When the whimper of welcome is stilled (how still!);
When the spirit that answered your every mood
Is gone-wherever it goes-for good,
You will discover how much you care
AND WILL GIVE YOUR HEART TO A DOG TO
TEAR.

Dogs as Companions

They are much superior to human beings as companions. They do not quarrel or argue with you. They never talk about themselves but listen to you while you talk about yourself, and keep up an appearance of being interested in the conversation. They never make stupid remarks and they never ask a young author with fourteen tragedies, sixteen comedies, several farces, and a couple of burlesques in his desk, why he doesn't write a play.

They never say unkind things. They never tell us our faults, "merely for our own good." They do not at inconvenient moments mildly remind us of our past follies and mistakes.

They never inform us, like our inamoratas sometimes do, that we are not nearly so nice as we used to be. We are always the same to them. He is very imprudent, a dog is. He never makes it his business to inquire whether you are in the right or in the wrong, never bothers as to whether you are going up or down upon life's ladder, never asks whether you are rich or poor, silly or wise, sinner or saint. You are his pal. That is enough for him, and come luck or misfortune, good repute or bad, honour or shame, he is going to stick to you, to comfort you, guard you, give his life for you, if need be-foolish, brainless, soulless dog! – *Jerome K. Jerome* in Idle Thoughts Of An Idle Fellow.

Fig. 106.—Mrs. F. M. Higgs's Black-and-tan Terrier Bagatelle.

Epitaph to a Dog
(On a monument in the garden of
Newstead Abbey, England)

NEAR THIS SPOT
ARE DEPOSITED THE REMAINS
OF ONE
WHO PSSESSED BEAUTY
WITHOUT VANITY,
STRENGTH WITHOUT INSOLENCE,
COURAGE WITHOUT FEROCITY,
AND ALL THE VIRTUES OF MAN
WITHOUT HIS VICES

THIS PRAISE, WHICH WOULD BE UNMEANING
FLATTERY
IFINSCRIBED OVER HUMAN ASHES,
IS BUT A JUST TRIBUTE TO THE MEMORY OF
"BOATSWAIN", A DOG
WHO WAS BORN AT NEWFOUNDLAND
MAY, 1803
AND DIED AT NEWSTEAD ABBEY
NOV. 18, 1808

When some proud son of man returns to earth,
Unknown to glory, but upheld by birth,
The sculptor's art exhausts the pomp of woe,
And storied urns record who rests below;
When all is done, upon the tomb is seen,
Not what he was, but what he should have been.
But the poor dog, in life the firmest friend,
The first to welcome, foremost to defend,

Whose honest heart is still his master's own,
Who labours, fights, lives breathes for him alone,
Unhonoured falls, unnoticed all his worth,
Denied in heaven the soul he held on earth-
While man, vain insect! hopes to be forgiven,
And claims himself a sole exclusive heaven.
Oh man! thou feeble tenant of an hour,
Debased by slavery, or corrupt by power-
Who knows thee well must quit thee with disgust,
Degraded mass of animated dust!
Thy love is lust, thy friendship all a cheat,
Thy smiles hypocrisy, thy words deceit!
By nature vile, ennobled but by name,
Each kindred brute might bid thee blush for shame.
Ye, who perchance behold this simple urn,
Pass on-it honours none you wish to mourn.
To mark a friend's remains these stones arise;
I never knew but one-and there he lies.

-LORD BYRON

Constancy

You don't need riches,
You don't need looks,
You needn't have read
A line in books,
You don't need purple,
You don't need fame-
Your dog will love you
Just the same!
You may lack money,
An ugly wight
Without the sense to
Come in at night,
You may be ragged,
And have no name-
Your dog will love you
Just the same!
                    -FRED B. MANN

A PROUD BOAST

I never barked when out of season;
I never bit without a reason;
I ne'er insulted weaker brother;
Nor wronged by force or fraud another.
Though brutes are placed a rank below,
Happy for man could he say so"
                    - BLACKLOCK

Little Dog Angel

High up in the courts of heaven today
     The little dog angel waits.
With the other angels he will not play
     But he sits alone at the gates.
For I know that my master will come, says he,
And when he comes he will call for me.
And his master, far in the world below,
     As he sits in his easy chair,
Forgets himself and whistles low
     For the dog-that is not there.
And the little dog angel cocks his ears
     And dreams that his master's voice he hears.
And I know, some day, when his master waits
     Outside in the dark and cold
For the hand of death to open the gates
     That lead to those courts of gold,
The little dog angel's eager bark
Will comfort his soul while he's still in the dark.

                  -NORAH M. HOLLAND

THE DOGLESS BOY

"But the poor dog, in life the firmest friend,
The first to welcome, foremost to defend.
Whose honest heart is still his master's own,
Who labours, fights, lives, breathes for him alone."

BYRON

Boy is used here in a generic sense, for the love
of animals, and especially dogs, is not confined to either
sex. We do not think a boy was ever born who, if
"entered" properly, would not love a dog and when
given the opportunity. There seems to be some affinity
between children and dogs. The selfish cat may be a
family pet, but its horizon of affection is usually filled
with a warm fireside and a saucer of milk and the claws
within the velvet are typical of its nature; uncertain of
temperament and cruel even in its seeming play. Not so
the dog. It matters not whether his lineage proclaims
him a blue blood or a mongrel, there is something
behind the eye of a dog which draws to the heart. No
animal is so responsive to the humanizing effect as the
dog. His idiosyncrasies and temperament are, like those
of man, much a matter of environment. Cuff him and
treat him generally as an Ishmael and he becomes one,
treat him like so many are in kennels nowadays, as a
mere chattel to be housed and fed as one of a number
and he becomes a mere automaton; but treat him as a
friend, as one of your household an dhow soon the
human influence is marked. His ideas are widened, his
intelligence develops and the many beautiful traits of a
confiding, honest nature which have earned him the title
of man's best friend, are brought to the surface. Though
the society of man has a humanizing effect on our four-

footed friends, the dog himself in no less manner, through his transparent temperament and honest actions may suggest and encourage the same traits in the budding nature of his little friend. Every boy should own a dog. Josh Billings well said that in the whole history of the world there is but one thing that money cannot buy, to wit: "The wag of a dog's tall." He might have added there is no animal on God's earth who, in the honesty of his affection, will still love and wag his tail for the hand which beats him. The love of Bill Sykes' dog for his brutal master is one of the sublimest thoughts Dickens ever conceived.

The boy who is raised with a dog for a "pal" is unwittingly humanized. The love for another is engendered in his heart, and afterward has its effect on his conduct in the wide world of mankind. Be his nature cruel, more from thoughtlessness than any inherent feeling, if he is a lad worth his salt he cannot but learn a lesson from the mild reproach of the brute he torments.

A horse would kick, a cat would bite or scratch under the same provocation; not so the dog. There are exceptions, of course, but no dog, we believe, is born savage; if he develops bad temper it is generally due to environment, and the parent's judgment must be exercised in providing the right sort of dog for the boy, as in other provisions for his welfare. A man may become a lover of dogs when manhood's cares and responsibilities place the dog on the same level as a favourite pipe. He has missed something. He will not "get into" his dog as he would have done as a boy. Once a dog lover always a dog lover, no matter whether the circumstances of his after life compel him to love them from afar. The dog is the better for it and so is the man. Buy your son a dog. – H. W. L.

LIEUT.-COLONEL C. S. DEAN'S BLACK-AND-TAN TERRIER CHAMPION STARKIE BEN

Pals

Hurrah!
Here they come!
Heralded loud by fife and drum,
The Boy and his Pal in proud parade!
The Boy is nonchalant, unafraid,
Heir of the Ages! Fronting life,
Ready to tilt with toil and strife.
And the Pal? He keeps his chum in sight,
Barking to left and barking to right,
And the two, as they march, proclaim to all,
"We are Boy and Dog, and Pal and Pal!"
Hurrah!
Watch them jog!
Wonderful creatures! Boy and Dog!

-SUSIE. H. BEST

The Little Black Dog

I wonder if Christ had a little black dog,
    All curly and woolly like mine,
With two long silk ears and a nose round and wet,
    And two eyes brown and tender that shine.
I'm sure if He had, that little black dog
    Knew right from the first He was God,
That he needed no proof that Christ was divine,
    But just worshipped the ground He trod.

I'm afraid that He hadn't, because I have Read Books
How He prayed in the Garden alone,
When all of His friends and disciples had fled,
Even Peter, that one called a stone.
And oh, I am sure that little black dog
With a true heart so tender and warm
Would never have left Him to suffer alone,
But creep right under His arm;
Would have licked those dear fingers in agony clasped,
And counting all favours but loss,
When they led Him way, would have trotted behind
And followed Him quite to the cross.
-ELIZABETH GARDNER REYNOLDS

Proverbs and Bits of Wisdom about Dogs

The more I see of men, the better I like my dog –
FREDERICK THE GREAT *(of his Italian greyhound)*.

"God created man; then seeing how weak he was, gave
him the dog." –TOUSSENEL.

For my part, I do with thou wert a dog, that I might love
thee. – SHAKESPEARE

Whenever a man is unhappy, God sends him a dog.
                                                    -LAMARTINE

Dog is the only animal that loves you more than he loves
himself – OLD SAYING

EPITAPH FOR A SMALL DOG

Here rests a little dog
    Whose feet ran never faster
Than when they took the path
    Leading to his master
        -LEBARON COOKE

EPITAPH ON A FAVOURITE DOG

Thou who passest on the path; if haply thout dost mark this monument, laugh not I pray thee, though it is a dog's grave; tears fell for me and the dust was heaped above me by a master's hands who likewise engraved these words on my tomb. – *From Greek literature (about 350 B.C)*

EPITAPH ON A DOG'S TOMBSTONE NEAR CHEVY CHASE, M.D., (1940)

"Dear Master:

I've explained to St. Peter, I'd rather stay here, outside of the pearly gates. I won't be a nuisance, I won't even bark. I'll be very patient and wait. I'll lie here and chew a celestial bone, no matter how long you may be. I miss you so much. If I went in alone, it wouldn't be heaven for me."

WHEN THE DOG'S SOUL COMES THROUGH HIS EYES

If a man does not soon pass beyond the thought "By what shall this dog profit me?" into the large state of simple gladness to be with dog, he shall never know the very essence of that companionship which depends not on the points of dog, but on some strange and subtle mingling of mute spirits. For it is by muteness that a dog becomes for one so utterly beyond value. With him one is at peace where words play no torturing tricks. When he just sits loving and knows that he is being loved, those are the moments that I think are precious to a dog: when, with his adoring soul coming through his eyes, he feels that you are really thinking of him.

– JOHN GALSWORTHY in Memories.

HOW BENVENUTO CELLINI'S DOG IDENTIFIED A ROBBER

Happening just about this time to pass by the square of Navona with my fine shock-dog, as soon as I came to the door of the city marshal, the dog barked very loudly and flew at a young man, who had been arrested by one Donnino, a goldsmith of Parma, formerly a pupil of Caradosso, upon suspicion of having committed a robbery. My dog made such efforts to tear this young fellow to pieces that he roused the city-guards.

The prisoner asserted his innocence boldly, and Donnino did not say so much as he ought to have done, especially as I was present. There happened likewise to be by one of the chief officers of the city-guard, who was a Genoese, and well acquainted with the prisoner's father; insomuch that on account of the violence offered by the dog, and for other reasons, they were for dismissing the youth, as if he had been innocent.

As soon as I came up, the dog, which dreaded neither swords nor sticks, again flew at the young man. The guards told me that if I did not keep off my dog they would kill it. I called off the dog with some difficulty, and as the young man was retiring, certain little paper bundles fell from under the cape of his cloak, which Donnino immediately discovered to belong to him.

Amongst them I perceived a little ring which I knew to be my property: whereupon I said: 'This is the villain that broke open my shop, and my dog knows him again.' I therefore let the dog loose, and he once more seized the thief, who then implored mercy, and told me he would restore me whatever he had of mine. On this I again called off my dog, and the fellow returned me all the gold, silver, and rings that he had robbed me of, and gave me five-and-twenty crowns over, imploring my forgiveness.

–BENVENUTO CELLINI
(from *Memoirs*, ending in 1562)

Rip Van Winkle's Dog Wolf

Rips sole domestic adherent was his dog Wolf, who was as much henpecked as his master; for Dame Van Winkle regarded them as companions in idleness, and even looked upon Wolf with an evil eye as the cause of his master's going so often astray. True it is, in all points of spirit befitting an honourable dog, he was as courageous an animal as ever scoured the woods – but what courage can withstand the ever-during and all-besetting terrors of a woman's tongue?

The moment Wolf entered the house, his crest fell, his tail drooped to the ground, or curled between his legs, he sneaked about with a gallows air, casting many a sidelong glance at Dame Van Winkle, and at the least flourish of a broomstick or ladle, he would fly to the door with yelping precipitation. . .

Poor Rip was at last reduced almost to despair, and his only alternative to escape from the labour of the farm and clamour of his wife, was to sometimes take gun in hand, and stroll away into the woods. Here he would sometimes seat himself at the foot of a tree, and share the contents of his wallet with Wolf, with whom he sympathized as a fellow-sufferer in persecution. 'Poor Wolf,' he would say, 'thy mistress leads thee a dog's life of it; but never mind, my lad, whilst I live thou shalt never want a friend to stand by thee'' Wolf would wag his tail, look wistfully in his master's face, and if dogs can feel pity, I verily believe he reciprocated the sentiment with all his hear.

– WASHINGTON IRVING (from *Rip Van Wingle*, in *The Sketch Book*), 1820.

By permission of *Our Dogs*

LIEUT.-COLONEL DEAN'S BLACK-AND-TAN
TERRIER BESWICK BEAUTY

THE DOG UNDER THE WAGON

"Come, wife," said good old farmer Gray,
"Put on your things, 'tis market day,
And we'll be off to the nearest town,
There and back ere the sun goes down.
Spot? No, we'll leave old Spot he whined,
And soon made up his doggish mind
      To follow under the wagon.

Away they went at a good round pace
And joy came into the farmer's face,
"Poor Spot," said he, "did want to come,
But I'm awful glad he's left at home –
He'll guard the barn, and guard the cot,
And keep the cattle out of the lot."
"I'm not so sure of that," thought Spot,
      The dog under the wagon.

The farmer all his produce sold
And go his pay in yellow gold:
Home through the lonely forest. Hark!
A robber springs from behind a tree;
"Your money or else your life," said he;
The moon was up, but he didn't see
      The dog under the wagon.

Spot ne'er barked and Spot ne'er whined
But quickly caught the thief behind;
He dragged him down in the mire and dirt,
And tore his coat and tore his shirt,
Then held him fast on the miry ground;
The robber uttered not a sound,

While his hands and feet the farmer bound,
    And tumbled him into the wagon.

So Spot he saved the farmer's life,
The farmer's money, the farmer's wife,
And now a hero grand and gay,
A silver collar he wears today;
Among his friends, among his foes –
And everywhere his master goes –
He follows on his horny toes,
    The dog under the wagon.
                - ANONYMOUS

QUESTIONS

Is there not something in the pleading eye
Of the poor brute that suffers, which arraigns
The law that bids it suffer? Has it not
A claim for some remembrance in the book
That fills its pages with the idle words
Spoken of man? Or is it only clay,
Bleeding and aching in the potter's hand,
Yet all his own to treat it as he will,
And when he will to cast it at his feet,
Shattered, dishonoured, lost for evermore?
My dog loves me, but could he look beyond
His earthly master, would his love extend
To Him who – hush! I will not doubt that He
Is better than our fears, and will not wrong
The least, the meanest of created things.
            - OLIVER WENDELL HOLMES

A FRIENDLY WELCOME

'Tis sweet to hear the watch-dog's honest bark
Bay deep-mouthed welcome as we draw near home;
'Tis sweet to know there is an eye will mark
Our coming, and look brighter when we come.
                                    - LORD BYRON

TO A DOG

On every side I see your trace;
Your water-trough's scarce dry;
Your empty collar in its place
Provokes the heavy sigh.

And you were here two days ago.
There's little changed, I see.
The sun is just as bright, but oh!
The difference to me!

The very print of your small pad
Is on the whitened stone.
Where, by what ways, or sad or glad,
Do you fare on alone?

Oh, little face, so merry-wise,
Brisk feet and eager bark!
The house is lonesome for your eyes,
My spirit somewhat dark.

Now, small, invincible friend, your love
Is done, your fighting o'er,
No more your wandering feet will rove
Beyond your own house-door.

The cats that feared, their hearts are high,
The dogs that loved will gaze
Long, long ere you come passing by
With all your jovial ways.

Th'accursed archer who has sent
His arrow all too true,
Would that his evil days were spent
Ere he took aim at you!

Your honest face, your winsome ways
Haunt me, dear little ghost,
And everywhere I see your trace,
Oh, well-beloved and lost!

        - ANONYMOUS

A BOY AND A DOG

I want my boy to have a dog
Or maybe two or three
He'll learn from them much easier
Than he would learn from me.
A dog will show him how to love
And bear no grudge or hate
I'm not so good at that myself
But dogs will do it straight.
I want my boy to have a dog
To be his pal and friend
So he may lean that friendship
Is faithful to the end.
There never yet has been a dog
Who learned to double-cross
Nor catered to you when you won
Then dropped you when you lost.

-Mary Hale, *The Old Spinner*

THROUGH SUNLIT FIELDS
(Poetical Reverie of a "Bird Dog" Man)

Through sunlit fields I sometimes stride
My stalwart pointers by my side.
The joy of life sings through each vein,
Who would not thrill to its refrain
While carefree roaming meadows wide,
The fall is o'er and now betide
On city sidewalks I must stride,
No more my pointers dash amain
Through sunlit fields.
But when in winters even'tide
I loll and doze by fire beside,
Imagination has free rein
And then I see myself again,
On mem'ries magic carpet ride
Through sunlit fields.

-EDWARD DANA KNIGHT

Rochelle Kennels, New Rochelle, N. Y.
BROOMFIELD SULTAN.

FOR A LITTLE BOY

I want to give a little boy-such an important little boy-something that will show him FAITH, alive and glowing.

I want to give a little boy something that will teach the spirit of him the glorious virtue of unselfish COURAGE.

I want to give a little boy something that will impress upon his clean heart and spirit every day, every night, every hour of the day and night the mighty power and exquisite beauty of LOVE.

I want to teach a little boy the importance of, and the reason for, DISCIPLINE.

And so=I am going to give a little boy a little dog, and what a gay and happy time a little boy and a little dog and a devoted dad will have! What a lovely and fascinating and interesting school we will attend-we three together! – R. A. Grady

"CHILDREN-DOG RECIPE"

Take on large grassy field,
One half-dozen children,
Two or three small dogs,
A pinch of brook
And some pebbles –
Mix the children and dogs, well together, then
put them in the field, stirring constantly. Pour the brook
over the pebbles. Sprinkle the field with flowers. Spread
over all a deep blue sky, and bake in the hot sun. When
brown, remove and set away in a bathtub to cool.

–Author unknown.

WHEN CAESAR MARCHED BEHIND HIS KING

When were kings compelled to march behind a
dog?

When King Edward VII of England died in
1910, it was learned he had given stern instructions that
his pet fox terrier named Caesar march directly behind
the artillery caisson carrying his body. Edward even
threatened to haunt any one who disobeyed this order.

And so it happened – Caesar marched behind
his master's body; and kings, potentates, prime ministers
and Emperor Kaiser Wilhelm of Germany marched
behind the little terrier.

Caesar himself lived to the ripe age of 14 years
and was buried in a bronze casket at Fort Rudd,
England.

ON THE ESSENTIAL ATTRIBUTES OF A DOG OWNER

Great Britain has an international reputation of being a nation of animal lovers. As recent statistics estimate the canine population of Britain to be approximately three million, while registrations at the Kennel Club are now in the region of 100,000 per year, there can be little doubt that we are a nation of dog owners. It is a sad fact, however, that in many cases these dogs are kept by owners who are far from being true animal lovers. It is still necessary for us to have a very active Royal Society for the Prevention of Cruelty to Animals; a fact which has often been commented upon to the writer by people abroad.

Happily, however, cases of downright physical cruelty to dogs, and to other animals, are rare in this country; but it is surprising how ignorant the average dog owner is, and the amount of cruelty through ignorance – incorrect, and over-, feeding, bad housing, continual "doseing", and insufficient exercise – to dogs is appalling. Many owners who would never beat a dog, and who would be most indignant if the truth was told them, are cruel to their dogs by habitually over-feeding them emotionally, as well as physically. There are also such thoughtless cruel acts as permitting small children to torment a dog, even if not inflicting physical pain, when the animal is not inclined to play.

This unconscious cruelty on the part of dog owners can be easily overcome by learning the correct principles of dog management, and an intelligent application of these principles without undue fussiness and sentimentality.

In becoming a dog owner certain responsibilities are undertaken, and the owner *must* be prepared to sacrifice something, if only in time and trouble, to the well-being of his pet, in the same way that married couples have to sacrifice a good deal of their pleasure when they undertake the responsibility of children.

It may be possible to keep a dog properly and in good health even in a bed-sitting room, provided one has the time to take him out, and in these circumstances it will be necessary much more frequently than with a dog kept in a large house with free access to a garden – but it would obviously be cruelty to keep, say, a large gun-dog under such conditions. If circumstances do not permit of a dog being kept properly, it is the *real* dog lover who refrains from keeping a dog until conditions change.

A sympathetic understanding of the dog – sloppy sentimentalism is *not* meant by this – is in-born in some people and can never be acquired by others, but it is possible for anyone to develop this to some extent or other. This is done by observation, a sensible love of dogs without undue "sloppiness", firmness without harshness, and by acquiring the knack of getting inside a dog's mind and understanding things from the dog's point of view. It is imperative that the dog's respect and trust should be gained by the owner; unfairness is a thing with a dog cannot understand and will never forgive. Unlimited patience and the strictest temper control on the part of the owner are essential, as are reliability, scrupulosity, regularity and method.

The ignorance on the part of dog owners, to which reference has been made, can best be overcome by practical instruction under a master of the subject, who, in addition, can impart his knowledge. As a practical course in dog management cannot possibly be undertaken by the majority of ordinary dog owners, the only alternative for them is to acquire as much knowledge as possible from books. But here a word of warning is necessary – it is essential that books on dogs should be read, and the advice given in them applied, with common sense. No book ever written can mention every possible contingency, and details vary with cases, but principles never vary, and if one has a good knowledge of sound principles of dog management and has taken the pains to develop the other attributes necessary in a dog owner, they can themselves readily adapt details to circumstances, and thereby give a fair deal to mankind's most responsive of companions – the Dog.

In a handbook of this nature, on a subject so large, it is only possible to give a brief outline; but it is to be hoped that the general facts explained will enable the owner to develop a sympathetic understanding of hi dog and the desire to seek more detailed knowledge from experienced friends, and from larger and more specialized books on the various aspects of dog management.

- CHARLES CASTLE

DOGS ON THE ROMAN FARM

Nor let the care of dogs be last in your thoughts; feed swift Spartan whelps and fierce Molossians alike on fattening whey. Never, which them on guard, need you fear in your stalls a midnight thief, nor onslaught of wolves, nor restless Spaniards behind your back. – Virgil – (From the *Georgies* III, trans. H. R. Fairclough), 30 B.C.

WHAT BREED WAS IT?

There is a certain strong breed of hunting-dogs, small, but worthy of a sublime song, which the wild tribes of painted Britons maintain, and they call them gaze-hounds. Their size, indeed, is about that of the worthless pampered domestic tabledogs, crooked, slight, shaggy, dull-eyed, but furnished with numerous envenomed teeth, and their feet armed with formidable nails.

The gaze-hound excels above all in his nose; he is first-rate for tracing, since he is very sagacious in finding the track of animals over the ground, and moreover, expert in indicating the very odour that floats in the air. –Oppian of Apamea (from *Cynegetica*, C. 215 A.D.)

'AWAY FROM CIVILIZATION, WHAT DOES ONE NEED MOST?'

If I had to spend a long time away from civilization and could take only one thing with me I would certainly take something alive, preferably a dog.

The reasons for this are because of his unwavering loyalty, his sense of responsibility as regards his master's person and belongings, his extremely acute sense of approaching danger and the absolute adoration that even a mongrel is capable of giving his owner.

More than anything alive, the dog seems to fill the need of a close affectionate honest friend. Therefore I would take a dog.

There is nothing in his mechanism to go static. There is nothing forced or mechanic about his feeling for you. There is no danger which hw ill not share willingly. He will never be disgustingly drunk. Neither will insist upon talking when you desire quiet. And no matter how soundly he may seem to be sleeping – if you need him he is right there every time.

I would take a dog because if, away from civilization, death should chance to be my lot, I could pass on happier in the knowledge that while life remained in his faithful body my dog would still be my champion, my defender. I am sure I would sleep the sweeter knowing that he was lying above me whispering "Peace, old pal, on the long, long trek."

"ON THE SLY"

One thing my wife and I've said over
And over-we will not feed Rover
At table, even though he begs
And nuzzles up against our legs
And toward us is forever turning
Those looks of hunger, hurt, and yearning...
We have agreed and that is why
We only do it on the sly.

-RICHARD ARMOUR.

THE HOME-LOVING DOG

The lonely fox roams far abroad,
On secret rapine bent, and midnight fraud;
Now haunts the cliff, now traverses the lawn,
And flies the hated neighbourhood of man:
While the kind spaniel, or the faithful hound,
Likest that fox in shape and species found,
Refuses through these cliffs and lawns to roam,
Pursues the noted path, and covets home;
Does with kind joy domestic faces meet,
Take what the glutted child denies to eat,
And, dying, licks his long-loved master's feet.

LOYALTY

(Reprinted from Dog World, 1924)

A man may lose his house and lot,
  His friends may pass him by,
He may not have a thin dime left
  To rent a slab of pie;

But if he owns the homeliest
  And saddest dog in town,
He has one pal whose honest love
  Will never turn him down.

A man may kick his mangy pup
  And cuss him day and night,
Still will the faithful cur be true
  And greet him with delight.

Life long he sits upon the porch
  And wags his happy tail,
To greet his lord when he shall come
  From Congress or from jail.

LIKE CHILD, LIKE PUPPY

Owning a dog is a serious responsibility. To enjoy the position of dog's master incurs obligation. The dog surrenders many of his natural rights and habits in return for the servitude he gives the human.

The puppy is the perfect example of trusting loyalty. To him the world's a stranger to be greeted. Not only each day but each moment of each hour of the day, he discovers something new in our world of humans, in which he must live.

Life is an endless chain experience of play, discovery and thrills. Not a care worries his carefree soul. What scene on this earth holds more pure happiness than that of a litter of playing puppies – brothers and sisters in a family world that has not yet known separation!

Consequently, a puppy, particularly if it is brought into a new home, should receive every consideration in the way of feeding, care, housing and training. At three months of age, it compares with the infant just out of the cradle; and to a great extent the same care which the child receives, should be given to the puppy.

GREAT FRIEND MAKER

Dale Carnegie, whose book How to Make Friends and Influence People has been a best seller, write: 'Why read my book to find out how to win friends?" Why not study the technique of the greatest winner of friends the world has ever known? You may meet him coming down the street. When you get within ten feet of him he will begin to wag his tail. If you stop and pat him he will almost jump out of his skin to show how much he likes you.

And you know that behind this show of affection on his part, there are no ulterior motives; he has nothing to sell and doesn't want to marry you.

"Did you ever stop to think that a dog is the only animal that does not have to work for a living? A hen has to lay eggs; a cow has to give milk; and a canary has to sing. But a dog makes his living by giving you nothing but love."

WALKING WITH A DOG HAS EXTRA PLEASURE

You will generally fare better to take your dog than invite your neighbour.

Your dog is a true pedestrian, and your neighbour is very likely a small politician. The dog enters thoroughly into the spirit of the enterprise; he is not indifferent or preoccupied; he is constantly sniffing adventure, laps at every spring, looks upon every field and wood as a new world to be explored, is ever on some fresh trail, knows something important will happen a little farther on, gazes with the true wonder-seeing eyes, whatever the spot or whatever the road, finds it good to be there – in short, is just that happy, delicious, excursive vagabond that touches one at so many points, and whose human prototype in a companion robs miles and leagues of half their power to fatigue. – JOHN BURROUGHS.

IF YOU CAN'T FIND THE PERFECT MAN, OWN A DOG

"And there is more than one woman – even a beautiful woman – who has never found the man to love the pilgrim soul in her; and, after passionate protestations and broken vows, old, disillusioned, sad, and deserted, she has regained faith in love and fidelity through the devotion of a dog.

"He does not change when beauty flees, nor when poverty comes, nor when health goes. He gives his heart, his true and single heart to his mistress forever.

"She may be old and grey, with furrowed face, but he sees the pilgrim soul in her. "

– Mrs. T. P. O'Connor in her book Dog Stars.

WHEN DACHS' EYES ARE DIM WITH LOVE

The dachshund's trusting eyes are dim
With love for you – and tender;
The dachshund is so long and slim
And slithery and slender
That when you pat his head on Sunday
His little tail won't wag till Monday
Hoot Mon! And also Teckelheil.
                    - BERTHA BRIGHT RAINGER

MY OLD HOUND PACK

When my hunting here is over
          From the tall harps' golden sounds
I will steal away to hearken
          To the voices of the hounds.
When they start a phantom red fox
          On a phantom heavenly hill,
And with me, a phantom huntsman,
          Getting all the old-time thrill.
For a man who's bred to hunting
          Must forever be that way;
And he'll never know it's heaven
          Till he listens' and can say:
'there's a short low tenor,
          And a yipping ki-hi;
There's a bell-mouth ringing

That a fox has got to dies.
There's a ding-dong chop-mouth,
    Always in the noise;
There's a bass with no bottom,
    And a rolling gong voice.
There's a bugle with a break,
    And a bugle with a scream,
And a high wailing tenor
    Like a trumpet in a dream!'
        -ARCHIBALD RUTLEDGE.

A PRAYER FOR ANIMALS

Hear our humble prayer O God for our friends the animals who are suffering – for all that are overworked, underfed and cruelly treated.

For any that are hunted, lost or deserted, frightened or hungry.

For all that are in pain or dying.

For all that must be put to sleep – we entreat for them Thy mercy and pity.

For all those who deal with them we ask a heart of compassion, gentle hands and kindly words.

Make us ourselves true friends of animals and may we share the blessings of the merciful for the sake of Thy Son – the tender hearted Healer – Jesus Christ our Lord, Amen!

THE DOG BELIEVED IN SIGNS

Ah! You should keep dogs – fine animals – sagacious creatures – dog of my own once – pointer – surprising instinct – out shooting one day – entering enclosure – whistled – dog stopped – whistled again – Ponto – nogo; stock still – called him – Ponto, Ponto – wouldn't move – dog transfixed – staring at a board – looked up; saw an inscription – "Gamekeeper has orders to shoot all dogs found in this enclosure" – wouldn't pass it – wonderful dog – valuable dog that – very. – Mr. Fingle, in Charles Dickens's Pickwick Paper.

CUVIER ON DOGS

"The domestic dog," said Cuvier, the great natural scientist, "is the most complete, the most singular, and the most useful conquest that man has gained in the animal world.

"The whole species has become our property; each individual belongs entirely to his master, acquires his disposition, knows and defends his property, and remains attached to until death; and all this, not through constraint or necessity, but purely by the influences of gratitude and real attachment.

"The swiftness, the strength, the sharp scent of the dog, have rendered him a powerful ally to man against the lower tribes, and were, perhaps, necessary for the establishment of the dominion of mankind over the whole animal creation. The dog is the only animal which has followed man over the whole earth."

MOTTO FOR A DOG HOUSE

I love this little house because
It offers, after dark,
A pause for rest, a rest for paws,
A place to moor my bark.
-Arthur Guiterman

REST IN PEACE

Father, in Thy starry tent,
I kneel, a humble suppliant,
A dog has died today on earth –
Of little worth
Yet very dear.
Gather him in Thy arms,
If only
For awhile,
I fear
He will be lonely,
Shield him with Thy smile.
-Wilfred J. Funk

OLD-FASHIONED ENGLISH TERRIERS.

THE LOVER OF DOGS

He made and loveth all.
　　Both man and bird and beast!
He prayeth best who loveth best
　　All things both great and small!
For the dear God who loveth us,
　　He made and loveth all.

-S. T. COLERIDGE.

LOYALTY

"You can't buy loyalty," they say;
I bought it though this very day.
You can't buy friendship, firm and true.
I bought sincerest friendship, too,
And truth and kindliness I got
And happiness, oh, such a lot,
So many joyous hours-to-be
Were sold with this commodity.

"I bought a life of simple faith
And love that will be mine till death;
And two brown eyes that I could see
Would not be long in knowing me.
I bought protection, I've a guard
Right now and ever afterward.
Buy human friendship? Maybe not –
You see, it was a dog I bought.

-Anne Campbell

SCOTCH DOG

A Scotsman had a dog, and each morning he gave him a penny to buy a bun. The dog deposited his penny each time in his kennel till he had five. Then off he went to the baker's shop and bought six buns for a shilling.

"MY PUP"

He's a rogue and a rascal,
A pest and a pain
And he wrecks my nylon hose.
He tracks up floors,
And nips at my heels
But I love him, goodness knows"
He annoys my friends,
When they come to call
With his shrill and noisy yap
And before they're settled in a chair
He lunges for a lap.
He simply ignores my mad protest,
And I am at a loss
It's plain for all my guests to see
Exactly who's the boss.
But when he comes at the end of day
And strikes a repentant pose,
I gather him up in my arms to rest
For I love him, goodness knows!

-HELENGA DARBY

AN XMAS PUP

A Poodle, a Yorkie
A chubby young Pug
A smart Pekingese
With his quaint little mug,
A Manchester toy
A Papillon rare,
A beloved tarrier
That's seen everywhere –
A Maltese, Affenpinscher
Whate'er it may be,
Take your choice,
But remember –
Put a pup 'neath your tree.
                    -PERLA O. RICHIARDS

GOING TO THE DOGS

My grandpa notes the world's worn cogs,
And says we're going to the dogs;
His granddad in his house of logs,
Swore things were going to the dogs;
His dad, among the Flemish bogs,
Vowed things were going to the dogs;
The caveman in his queer skin togs,
Said things were going to the dogs;
But this is what I wish to state –
The dogs have had an awful wait.
                    -Anonymous.

MONGREL PUP FROM THE DOG SHOP

"The months crept by, as seasons will, the pup
     Grew lank, unlovely as a clump of weeds;
And as he grew, our wonder grew in kind,
     That one lone dog could boast so many breeds.
He had an airedales's face but that was all;
     The bagging ears were those of any hound;
His silken coat was eloquent of collie;
     And from his tail we knew where he'd been
found."

         -MAURICE J. RONAYNE

A PROBLEM

What dog to buy?
Which breed to try?
I ponder and ponder –
I worry and sigh!
Long hair? Short hair?
Eyes deep brown, or yellow?
A hunter or collier –
Or just a good fellow?
Do I want a companion,
A guardian – a ratter?
A lap dog to cuddle?
Oh, what does it matter!
Big breed, small breed –
Black, white or brown.
I want a dog
For my very own! -NAN SWIGERT

CHRISTMAS PUPPIES

Every single puppy here
        Is saying: "Choose me!"
Wagging tail, wiggling ears, -
        "Don't refuse me!
"I'm your dog, wide awake!
        Won't we have fun?"
Well, we have got to take
        Every single one!
           -NANCY BYRD TURNER

IN RETROSPECT

Our house is empty, silent now –
I never knew just how
A little dog could fill a place,
Scampering through at breakneck pace,
Scattering rugs – an upset chair –
Confusion reigned most everywhere.
But what I'd give if it could be
That he again would meet and jump on me
           - Capt. Ellis Reed-Hill

Napoleon in Exile Recalls an Incident of the Retreat from Moscow

Suddenly I saw a dog coming out from under the clothes of a corpse. He rushed forward toward us and then returned t his retreat, uttering mournful cries. He licked the face of his master and darted toward us again; it seemed as if he was seeking aid and vengeance at the same time.

Whether it was my state of m ind, or the place, the times, the weather, the act itself, or I know not what, never has anything, on all my fields of battle, made such an impression upon me. I stopped involuntarily to contemplate the spectacle; that man, I said to myself, perhaps has friends, perhaps he has them in the camp, in his company, and yet he lies here abandoned by all except his dog.

What is man! and what the mystery of his impressions! I had ordered battles without emotion, battles which were to decide the fate of the army; I had seen, dry-eyed, movements executed which brought about the loss of a great number of our soldiers; here I was moved to tears. What is certain is that at the moment I must have been more favourably disposed toward a suppliant enemy. I better understood Achilles surrendering Hector's body to Priam's tears.

SCOTLAND'S BURNS ON DOGS

Man is the god of the dog; he knows no other; he can understand no other. And see how he worships him! With what reverence he crouches at his feet, with what love he fawns upon him! With what dependence he looks up to him! With what cheerful alacrity he obeys him!

His whole soul is wrapt up in his god! All the powers and faculties of his nature are devoted to his service! And these powers and faculties are ennobled by the intercourse.

Divines tell us that it just ought to be so with Christians – but the dog puts the Christian to shame

– ROBERT BURNS.

SCOTTISH NOVELIST ON DOGS

The Almighty who gave the dog to be the companion of our pleasures and our trials, hath invested him with a nature noble and incapable of deceit. He forgets neither friend nor foe, remembers with accuracy both benefit and in fury, and hath a share of man's intelligence but no share of man's falsehood.

– SIR WALTER SCOTT

TO BLANCO

My dear, dumb friend, low-lying there,
  A willing vassal at my feet,
Glad partner of my home and fare,
  My shadow in the street,

I look into your great, brown eyes,
Where love and loyal homage shine,
And wonder where the difference lies
  Between your soul and mine.

For all of good that I have found
  Within myself, or human kind,
Hath royally informed and crowned
  Your gently heart and mind.

I scan the whole broad earth around
For that one heart which, real and true,
Bears friendship without end or hound,
  And find the prize in you.

I trust you as I trust the stars;
Nor cruel loss, nor scoff, nor pride,
Nor beggary, nor dungeon bars,
  Can move you from my side.

A DOG AND A MAN

He was a dog
       But he stayed at home
       And guarded the family night and day.

He was a dog
       That didn't roam.
       He lay on the porch or chased the stray –
       The tramps, the burglar, the hen, away;
       For a dog's true heart for that household beat
       At morning and evening, in cold and heat.
He was a dog.

He was a man,
       And didn't stay
       To cherish his wife and his children fair.

He was a man.
       And every day
       His heart grew callous, its love-beats rare,
       He thought of himself at the close of day.
       And, cigar in his fingers, hurried away
       To the club, the lodge, the store, the show.
       But – he had a right to go, you know.
He was a man.

- ANONYMOUS

ARGUS

When wise Ulysses, from his native coast
Long kept by wars, and long by tempests tost,
Arrived at last – poor, old, despised, alone,
To all his friends, and e'en his queen, unknown,
Changed as he was, with age, and toils, and cares,
Furrowed his rev'rend face, an d white his hairs,
In his own palace forced to ask his bread,
Scorned by those slaves his former bounty fed,
Forgot of all his own domestic crew,
His faithful dog his rightful master knew!
Unfed, unhoused, neglected, on the clay
Like an old servant, now cashiered, he lay;
And though ev'n then expiring on the plain,
Touched with resentment of ungrateful man,
And longing to behold his ancient lord again,
Him when he saw, he rose, and crawled to meet
('Twas all he could), and fawned and kissed his feet,
Seized with dumb joy; then falling by his side,
Owned his returning lord, looked up, and died.

-ALEXANDER POPE

THE
BLACK AND TAN TERRIER.

ADVICE TO A DOG

Say truth good dogge, and doe not spare to barke,
But snarle and snappe at every sneaking thief,
Let not a Curre goe leering in the darke,
But shew thy kind, bough like a dogge, be briefe;
Lie at the door, give warning to the house,
Scratch at a flea, but care not for a louse.

Nicollo Machiavelli

(1469-1527)

PHILOSPHERS

The dogs are God's philosophers –
Though oft beset by fleas,
Because the masters, whom they love,
Eliminate not these.

Where things reversed, the human folk,
Infected with like 'bores',
Man's world were filled with dissonance,
At pain the dog ignores.

Ye-praters of real consequence,
Ye human folk 'divine'
Or so you think, forget ye not
To note a doggie's whine.

-Madge Acton Mansfield

QUOTES FROM LITERATURE

SHAKESPEARE ON DOGS

I had rather a dog and bay the moon. – Shakespeare

Cry 'havoc' and let slip the dogs of war. – Shakespeare

You play the spaniel and think with the wagging of your
tongue to win me. – Shakespeare

Like Hercules himself, do what he may,
The cat will mew and dog will have his day. –
Shakespeare

> Mastiff, greyhound, mugril grim,
> Hound or spaniel, brache or lym,
> Or bobtail tike, or trundle tail.
> Shakespeare's King Lear – III-6

> My hounds are bred out of the Spartan kind . .
> and their heads are hung
> With ears that sweep away the morning dew
> Shakespeare's Midsummer Night's Dream 4-1

ITALIAN PROVERBS ON CANE (DOG)

Every dog is lion in his own house.
Cut off a dog's tail and he is still a dog.
Where there are no dogs, the fox is king.
A good dog and a good wife stay at home.

German proverb – he that represents himself as a dog must also bark like a dog.

ST. ROCHE – patron saint of dogs, on his deathbed. (13th century)

A soft caress fell on my cheek,
My hands were thrust apart.
And two big sympathizing eyes
Gazed down into my heart.

And of St. Roche's death:

Exempt from blame, he gave up his soul
As a good Christian, in the arms of his dog.

DOGGY ADVICE IN DOGGEREL

I've led a wild life;
I've earned what I've spent;
I've paid all I've borrowed;
I've lost all I've lent,
I loved a woman –
That came to an end;
Get a good dog, boys,
He'll be your real friend
ANONYMOUS

DOGGEREL

A man may smile and bid you hail,
Yet wish you to the devil;
But when a good dog wags his tail,
You know he's on the level.
                    - ANONYMOUS

TRIBUTE TO A SPANISH BREED

The great Pyrenees is a huge-sized dog, now fully
recognised in dog shows throughout the world, yet
seldom receives the praises due him. Here is an excerpt
from the Shepherd Dog of the Pyrenees, written by
ELLEN MURRAY.

When day at last
Broke, and the grey fog lifted, there I saw
On that ledge, against the dawning light,
My little one asleep, sitting so near
That edge that as I looked his red barette
Fell from his nodding head down the abyss.
And there, behind him, crouched Pierrot; his teeth,
His good, strong teeth, clenching the jacket brown,
Holding the child in safety. With wild bounds
Swift as the grey wolf's own I climbed the steep,
And as I reached them Pierrot beat his tail,
And looked at me, so utterly distressed.
With eyes that said: "Forgive, I could not speak,'
But never loosed his hold till my dear rogue
Was safe within my arms.

DOG BECOMES 'FIRST FRIEND'

And the woman said: 'His name is not Wild
Dog any more, but the First Friend, because he will be
our friend for always and always and always.'
-From one of Rudyard Kipling's stories.

MY COMFORTER

The world had all gone wrong that day
And tired and in despair,
Discouraged with the ways of life,
I sank into my chair.

A soft caress fell on my cheek,
My hands were thrust apart.
And two big sympathizing eyes
Gazed down into my heart.

I had a friend; what cared I now
For fifty worlds? I knew
One heart was anxious when I grieved –
My dog's heart, loyal, true.

"God bless him, " breathed I soft and low,
And hugged him close and tight.
One lingering lick upon my ear
And we were happy – quite.

- ANONYMOUS

THE DEAD BOY'S PORTRAIT AND HIS DOG

Day after day I have come and sat
Beseechingly upon the mat,
Wistfully wondering where you are at.

Why have they placed you on the wall,
So deathly still, so strangely tall?
You do not turn from me, nor call.

Why do I never hear my name?
Why are you fastened in a frame?
You are the same, and not the same.

Away from me why do you stare
So far out in the distance where
I am not? I am here! Not there!

What has your little doggie done?
You used to whistle me to run
Beside you, or ahead, for fun!

You used to pat me, and a glow
Of pleasure through my life would go!
How is it that I shiver so?

My tail was once a waving flag
Of welcome. Now I cannot wag
It for the weight I have to drag.

I know not what has come to me.
'Tis only in my sleep I see
Things smiling as they used to be.

I do not dare to bark; I plead
But dumbly, and you never heed;
Nor my protection seem to need.

I watch the door, I watch the gate;
I am watching early, watching late,
Your doggie still! – I watch and wait.

- GERALD MASSEY

Extract from '*The Tale of Your Dog – His Origin and Need*'

Dogs are essentially gentle beings, and our imagination
as well as our eyes, if only we will use them, should
convince us that because of their capacity for sharing our
moods and occupations, and thorough their ability to
give expression to the inner workings of their minds,
they are above all other animals destined to be our
friends. Indeed, it is we who are in many respects the
richer by this friendship. For in his dignity and
command of temper; in his wisdom and patience; in his
loyalty; and above all in his selflessness, a dog is a very
prince of gentlemen.

– MITFORD BRICE

Material in this book has been sourced from the following titles:

J. H. Walsh. *The Dogs Of The British Islands*. 1867
Vero Shaw. *The Illustrated Book Of The Dog*. 1879
Rawdon B. Lee. *A History And Description Of The Modern Dogs*. 1894
H. W. Huntington. *My Dog And I*. 1897
H. W. Huntington. *The Show Dog*. 1901
C. H. Lane. *Dog Shows And Doggy People*. 1902
W, D. Drury. *British Dogs - Their Points, Selection, And Show Preparation*. 1903
Herbert Compton. *The Twentieth Century Dog*. 1904
James Watson. *The Dog Book - A Popular History Of The Dog*. 1906
J. Sidney Turner. *The Kennel Encyclopaedia*. 1907
Robert Leighton. *The New Book Of The Dog*. 1907
J. Maxtee. *British terriers: Their Breeding, Management And Training*. 1909
Pierce O'conor. *Terriers For Sport*. 1922
A. Croxton Smith. *About Our Dogs - The Breeds And Their Management*. 1931
Stanley West. *The Book Of Dogs*. 1935

Lightning Source UK Ltd.
Milton Keynes UK
UKOW051813090312

188670UK00001B/157/P